DEEP INCARNATION

Duffy Lectures in Global Christianity
Boston College

Latin American Theology: Roots and Branches
Maria Clara Bingemer

Religion and Faith in Africa: Confessions of an Animist
Agbonkhianmeghe E. Orobator, SJ

*A Theology of Southeast Asia: Liberation-Postcolonial
Ethics in the Philippines*
Agnes M. Brazal

Deep Incarnation: God's Redemptive Suffering with Creatures
Denis Edwards

DEEP INCARNATION

God's Redemptive Suffering with Creatures

DENIS EDWARDS

ORBIS BOOKS

www.orbisbooks.com

ORBIS BOOKS
Maryknoll, New York 10545

Fathers and Brothers
MARYKNOLL

Founded in 1970, Orbis Books endeavors to publish works that enlighten the mind, nourish the spirit, and challenge the conscience. The publishing arm of the Maryknoll Fathers and Brothers, Orbis seeks to explore the global dimensions of the Christian faith and mission, to invite dialogue with diverse cultures and religious traditions, and to serve the cause of reconciliation and peace. The books published reflect the views of their authors and do not represent the official position of the Maryknoll Society. To learn more about Maryknoll and Orbis Books, please visit our website at www.maryknollsociety.org.

Library of Congress Cataloging-in-Publication Data

Names: Edwards, Denis, 1943– author.
Title: Deep incarnation : God's redemptive suffering with creatures / Denis Edwards.
Description: Maryknoll, NY : Orbis Logo, [2019] | Series: Duffy lectures in global Christianity | Includes bibliographical references and index. | Description based on print version record and CIP data provided by publisher; resource not viewed.
Identifiers: LCCN 2019003405 (print) | LCCN 2019009824 (ebook) | ISBN 9781608337941 (ebook) | ISBN 9781626983304 (pbk.)
Subjects: LCSH: Incarnation—History of doctrines. | Creation. | Salvation—Christianity.
Classification: LCC BT220 (ebook) | LCC BT220 .E39 2019 (print) | DDC 231.7—dc23
LC record available at https://lccn.loc.gov/2019003405

Contents

SERIES FOREWORD

Duffy Lectures in Global Christianity

Richard Gaillardetz

For some decades now we have witnessed a growing acknowl-edgment of the global character of Christianity. As we appre-ciate more and more the diverse forms that Christianity has taken over the past two millennia, it has become clear that Christian theology can no longer afford to heed only those theological voices that have originated from North America and Western Europe. As one of the most famous of those West-ern European voices, Karl Rahner, famously admitted, for too long the church had functioned as

> an export firm which exported a European religion as a commodity it did not really want to change but sent throughout the world together with the rest of the cul-ture and civilization it considered superior.[1]

Yet the Second Vatican Council acknowledged the ways in which the Word of God has been planted as a seed in the local

---

[1] Karl Rahner, "A Basic Theological Interpretation of Vatican II," in *Concern for the Church* [*Theological Investigations*, vol. 20], (New York: Crossroad, 1981), 78.

soil of diverse sociocultural regions and given birth to fresh expressions of the faith.[2]

Since the council, the Christian church has only grown in its appreciation for the value of diverse, deeply inculturated expressions of the one faith. These expressions might appear in the form of local liturgies and spiritualities, or in distinctive religious customs and popular devotions. Among these diverse expressions, we must include theological articulations of the faith that arise as Christians bring the Gospel into critical conversation with a distinct set of questions and concerns particular to their local context. The church universal is enriched when these voices can be heard, not only in their own sociocultural context, but by the churches throughout the *communio ecclesiarum*.

This growing recognition of the wonderful diversity evident within global Christianity has brought to consciousness the urgent need to provide platforms from which the diversity of theological voices can be heard throughout the church. Among the wide range of religious publishers, Orbis Books has stood out because of its long-standing commitment to give voice to the insights and concerns of local churches throughout the world.

In the sphere of academia, Boston College's Theology Department has also recognized the urgent need to expand academic theological formation and conversation to explicitly include theological voices from beyond North America and Western Europe. It is with that commitment in mind that in 2015 the Boston College Theology Department established an annual lecture series devoted to an exploration of Global Christianity. These annual lectures are dedicated to the memory of Fr. Stephen Duffy (1931–2007), who taught systematic theology at Loyola University in New Orleans from 1971 to 2007, and whose career was dedicated in no small part to the

---

[2] The Second Vatican Council, "The Decree on the Missionary Activity of the Church" (*Ad Gentes*), article 22.

universal reach of God's grace and the embodiment of that grace in diverse religious and cultural forms.

Each year Boston College invites an internationally recognized scholar from a different continent to give a series of five lectures on a topic of their choosing. The goal of these lectures is to broaden the theological conversation both at Boston College and for the church at large. Each set of lectures is published in a volume in cooperation with Orbis Books. Past Duffy Lecturers have included Maria Clara Bingemer, Agbonkhianmeghe E. Orobator, SJ, and Agnes M. Brazal.

Preface

Niels Henrik Gregersen

Denis Edwards belongs to the rare breed of contemporary theologians who at once are rooted in a calm spiritual presence while persistently looking for new theological ways of explaining what the Christian faith is all about, and why it matters—for us and for our contemporaries.

When I was still a young theologian, I knew Denis Edwards's name from his contributions to the dialogue between theology and the natural sciences. Even then I detected two ways in which he stood out from most scholars in the field. One thing was that his interest in the sciences was not only about science per se, but just as much about broadening the horizon of his own theological perspective; his own tradition was at play and in principle at risk, but it was also part of the game.

Another thing was the practical approach he took to science as well as theology. This came to the fore in the first book I read by him, *Ecology at the Heart of Faith: The Change of Heart That Leads to a New Way of Living on Earth* (Orbis Books, 2006). I was surprised to find that Denis had a keen understanding of the relevance of "deep incarnation" for eco-theology, a field that had hitherto mostly been framed in the context of a theology of creation. I have to thank Denis for discovering that the proposal of deep incarnation was not only about evolutionary thinking but also about ecological thinking—

about how to rescue a flourishing and inhabitable planet from too linear, too anthropocentric ways of thinking. So I found in him a kind of kindred spirit, even though we lived far apart from each other, in Australia and Denmark, and only meet occasionally.

One of those occasions was a science-and-religion conference in the Bay Area hosted by the Center for Theology and the Natural Sciences. We went out for dinner in San Francisco Harbor and talked about deep incarnation among many other things. I expressed my wish to one day collect a group of creative and critical thinkers around a deepening of Christology. At the end of the dinner (when I had already forgotten about it), Denis concluded with his deep voice: "Niels, I think you should go for it." And so it went. Some years later, in 2011, it became real in Hamlet's Elsinore due to substantial help from the John Templeton Foundation, and we again became part of a common publication.

In his new book Denis Edwards offers several things. First, he gives us very fair and precise analyses of the ramifications of the different aspects of deep incarnation and of the main proponents involved. But as always, Denis also does something more. Although Athanasius, Bonaventure, and Martin Luther have been dealt with before, Denis Edwards leads us back to the second-century Church Father Irenaeus. In a sense, Irenaeus gave the birth-seed of what was later to develop into Eastern and Western traditions—and later again into Catholic and Protestant tradition. The interrelation between creation theology, Christology, and pneumatology in expressing the deep divine involvement in our corporeal world carries with it clear parallels with central aspects of the proposal of deep incarnation. Through this new volume, we know why.

Likewise, at the other end of the spectrum, Denis Edwards offers an analysis of the evolutionary theology of Karl Rahner, who has already shaped a substantial part of modern Roman Catholic theology. Now suddenly, it appears to what extent common concerns emerge between a Protestant theologian writing on Luther and an almost-contemporary giant such as Karl Rahner.

I recommend that laypeople concerned about the relation between Christ and evolution and ecology should read Denis Edwards's new theological book. Also, I advise the reader to be aware of why Denis Edwards insists on taking time as seriously as space in expressing the broad-scale Christology of deep incarnation. For the actual Jesus story, enacted in time and space, should be the basis for any future Christology—deep, or skin-deep.

Niels Henrik Gregersen
University of Copenhagen

Introduction

There are two interrelated reasons for taking up the theme of deep incarnation in this book. The first is the widely felt need to explore the Christological grounding for Christian ecological theology. It asks the question: What relationship is there between the wider natural world, the world of galaxies and stars, mountains and seas, bacteria, plants and animals, and the life, death, and resurrection of Jesus Christ? When ecological theology emerged during the second half of the twentieth century, there was a tendency to focus on creation theology, in isolation from the theology of incarnation and redemption. After all, it was thought, since the Reformation both Protestant and Roman Catholic theologies have been so preoccupied with human redemption as to leave no theological room for other creatures. While in the Christian East the threefold interrelationship between God, human beings, and the wider creation, found in the Scriptures and Patristic writers, had been maintained, the wider creation had been largely dropped in the West. The focus had been almost exclusively on humans and God, and particularly on human redemption in Christ.

It is understandable, then, that some ecological theology and spirituality responded with a focus on creation theology, at times in a blending of creation spirituality and popular science, as in the "new story" of the universe.[1] Although these

---

[1] Thomas Berry, *The Dream of the Earth* (San Francisco: Sierra Club Books, 1988); Brian Swimme and Thomas Berry, *The Universe Story: From the Primordial Flaring Forth to the Ecozoic Age—A Celebration of the Unfolding of the Cosmos* (San Francisco: HarperSanFrancisco, 1984).

efforts have been fruitful, leading to a new vision and a deepened commitment to the natural world, in some expressions of these approaches at the popular level, the prioritizing of creation theology over salvation theology has left little or no place for the incarnation and salvation in Christ.

A little theological reflection, however, makes clear that a fully Christian approach to the natural world cannot be limited to the theology of creation in isolation, but must also involve salvation in Christ. The theological meaning of mountains, seas, animals, plants, the climate of our planet, the Milky Way Galaxy, and the observable universe will involve the whole story of God's self-bestowal to creatures in creation, incarnation, and final transfiguration. The problem with the Western church's focus on redemption is not its concern with salvation, but that it has too often limited itself to human salvation, often in a highly individualistic way. What is needed is not a sidelining of salvation in Christ, but an enormous extension in the recent Western understanding of it, so that, faithful to the biblical promises of a new heavens and a new earth, salvation can be seen to involve the whole creation.[2]

A second closely related reason for taking up the theme of deep incarnation is the need for a theological response to the loss and suffering that is such an intrinsic part of an evolutionary view of the world. A contemporary awareness of the 3.7-billion-year history of life's evolution on our planet enormously amplifies the ancient problem of evil, not only because of the vastly increased scale of the loss, pain, and death involved, but also because it has now become clear that these costs are intrinsic to the evolutionary processes

---

[2] Ernst Conradie led an international ecumenical group that worked cooperatively on this issue for five years, resulting in a series of publications, including Ernst Conradie, ed., *Creation and Salvation, Volume 1, A Mosaic of Selected Classic Christian Theologies* (Zurich: LIT, 2012), and *Creation and Salvation, Volume 2, A Companion on Recent Theological Movements* (Zurich: LIT, 2012).

that give rise to the flourishing and diversity of life—they are built-in. The response of some in the past, making human sin responsible, will not work in this new context, where modern humans appear very late in the story of evolution—about 200,000 years ago. This seems to leave the Creator responsible for creating in a way that is very costly. The second theological question, then, is: How can we think of the good, generous, and loving God of biblical faith in relationship to the costs of evolution?

In the light of God's self-giving and self-revelation in Christ, this question can be focused on the life, death, and resurrection of Jesus of Nazareth: What relation is there between the suffering, predation, extinction, loss, and death that are found in the natural world and the incarnation of God in Jesus Christ? It is important to note at the beginning of this discussion that, in this book and in the work of theologians discussed here, incarnation does not refer simply to the birth of Jesus, but to the whole event of the Word of God becoming flesh, to every aspect of Jesus's material and bodily existence, and to his whole life and ministry that culminates in his death and resurrection.

It is in this context that Danish theologian Niels Gregersen introduced the language of *deep incarnation* seeking to show the radical meaning of the incarnation, and specifically of the cross of Christ, for suffering creatures. He proposes that "the incarnation of God in Christ can be understood as a radical or 'deep' incarnation, that is, an incarnation into the very tissue of biological existence, and system of nature."[3] He sees the cross as God's identification with creation in its evolutionary

---

[3] Niels Henrik Gregersen, "The Cross of Christ in an Evolutionary World," *Dialog: A Journal of Theology* 40 (2001): 192–207, at 205; See also Gregersen, "Deep Incarnation: Why Evolutionary Continuity Matters in Christology," *Toronto Theological Journal* 26, no. 2 (2010): 173–88; and Gregersen, ed., *Incarnation: On the Scope and Depth of Christology* (Minneapolis: Fortress Press, 2015).

emergence, and as an icon and microcosm of God's redemptive presence to all creatures in their suffering and death.

The concept of deep incarnation has since been taken up by other theologians, including Elizabeth Johnson, Celia Deane-Drummond, Christopher Southgate, and Richard Bauckham, who have made use of it in their own distinctive ways.[4] I describe their work along with that of Gregersen in the opening chapter of this book, which outlines some of the recent work on deep incarnation. Then, in the next three chapters, I seek to further explore deep incarnation by bringing it into dialogue with the incarnational theology of three great theologians: Irenaeus of Lyons from the second century, Athanasius of Alexandria from the fourth, and Karl Rahner from the twentieth. In the last chapter I offer my own understanding of the theology of deep incarnation in the light of these explorations.

An important moment in the recent story of deep incarnation was the symposium on this theme held at Elsinore, Denmark, in August 2011. This richly ecumenical and collaborative gathering was sponsored by the John Templeton Foundation with the support of the Faculty of Theology at Copenhagen University. It was convened by Dr. Mary Ann

---

[4] Deep incarnation has also played a significant role in my own theology. See Denis Edwards, *Ecology at the Heart of Faith* (Maryknoll, NY: Orbis Books, 2006), 52–64; "'Every Sparrow That Falls to the Ground': The Cost of Evolution and the Christ-Event," *Ecotheology* 11, no. 1 (March 2007): 103–23; *Partaking of God: Trinity, Evolution, and Ecology* (Collegeville, MN: Liturgical Press, 2014), 54–67; "Incarnation and the Natural World: Explorations in the Tradition of Athanasius," in Gregersen, *Incarnation: On the Scope and Depth of Christology*, 157–76; "Sublime Communion: The Theology of the Natural World in *Laudato Si'*," *Theological Studies* 77 (June 2016): 377–91; "Key Issues in Ecological Theology: Incarnation, Evolution, Communion," in *Theology and Ecology across the Disciplines: On Care for Our Common Home*, ed. Celia Deane-Drummond and Rebecca Artinian-Kaiser (London: Bloomsbury, 2018), 65–78.

Meyers of the Templeton Foundation and Niels Henrik Gregersen of Copenhagen University. The book that springs from, and builds on, this symposium is an important resource for the theology of deep incarnation.[5] Another such resource is found in Gregersen's lectures along with the responses of other scholars offered in the J. K. Russell Lectures, at the Center for Theology and the Natural Sciences, Berkeley, in 2013.[6] Niels Gregersen has recently offered a lecture series on deep incarnation at The Goshen College Conference on Religion and Sciences of 2017, and I have given the 2018 Duffy Lectures at Boston College on the same theme.

This book has its origins in the Duffy Lectures. I am deeply grateful to Richard Gaillardetz, Chair of the Theology Department, and to the wider theological community at Boston College, for the invitation to offer this series, and for their warm welcome and generous engagement with me and my work. It was an honor for me to take up this series named after Stephen Duffy, a theologian whose work I have long admired. I am grateful not only to Rick Gaillardetz for his generosity and warm hospitality, and to Mary Ann Hinsdale and the participants in the doctoral seminar she led built around the lectures, but also to all those faculty and students who engaged with me in the lectures and greatly enriched my thinking about the meaning of the incarnation. I was privileged to stay on campus with the Jesuit community at St. Mary's Hall. It was a joy to share meals, conversations, and Eucharist with them, and I am deeply thankful for their hospitality and the opportunity to participate in their community life.

Robert Ellsberg, editor of Orbis Books, warmly encouraged me in the transition from a series of lectures to this book, and I am delighted to be working with him and all the staff at Orbis Books in this production. I am very grateful to my colleagues

---

[5] Gregersen, *Incarnation: On the Scope and Depth of Christology.*

[6] For the J. K. Russell lectures and responses, see *Theology & Science* 11, no. 4 (2013): 370–468.

who have read the manuscript and given me critical comments and a great deal of support, particularly to James McEvoy and Patricia Fox, RSM. Bible quotations are from the NRSV translation.

I

Deep Incarnation in Recent Theology

The concept of deep incarnation was first articulated in a 2001 article by Danish Lutheran theologian Niels Henrik Gregersen. In this chapter I begin by outlining Gregersen's original expression of deep incarnation as a theological response to the pain, extinction, and death that are part of evolutionary emergence. Then I describe briefly how four evolutionary and ecological theologians have taken up this concept: Elizabeth A. Johnson, Celia Deane-Drummond, Christopher Southgate, and Richard Bauckham. Then, in the last section, I trace how Gregersen's thinking on deep incarnation has developed in some of his later publications.

Niels Gregersen on the Theology of Deep Incarnation

Niels Gregersen's original article on deep incarnation builds on, and seeks to extend, Martin Luther's theology of the cross, in order to address the costs that contemporary science shows to be part and parcel of evolutionary emergence.[1] Gregersen

---

[1] Niels Henrik Gregersen, "The Cross of Christ in an Evolutionary World," *Dialog: A Journal of Theology: A Journal of Theology* 40, no. 3 (Fall 2001): 192–207.

asks himself the question: If God's way of creating occurs through natural selection with all its built-in costs, "how can the Christian belief in the mercy of God be consonant with the ruthlessness of evolutionary processes?"[2] He seeks a contemporary theology of the cross that can offer a response to the widespread suffering and loss that are intrinsic to an evolutionary world.

Gregersen develops his theological response in two steps. First, he proposes that both the pain and the joy of creaturely existence are to be understood as part of the evolutionary "package deal" of God's creation of a universe of finite creatures.[3] Biological death is not due to human sin, but existed millions of years before the emergence of *Homo sapiens*. Death is part of the process of nature's creativity: it is "one way through which God creates novelty in evolution."[4] Pain can be understood as "the price paid for having a highly sensitive nervous system."[5] The capacity for mental suffering can be seen as the price paid for an evolved consciousness, capable of calculating various options and outcomes.

Gregersen thinks that while evolutionary biology sharpens the problem of theodicy, making it plain that death and pain are intrinsic to an evolutionary world, and that they cannot be explained simply by human sin, it can also offer the beginning of a response to this problem. An evolutionary worldview can provide a basis for a modest theodicy, precisely because it sees our evolved world as a package deal, in which there can be no capacity for experiencing the joys of existence without also experiencing its pains. In an evolutionary view, pain has a positive evolutionary function, increasing the attentiveness and adaptive fitness of organisms, and death is essential for the cycle of generations that make evolution possible.

---

[2] Ibid., 192.

[3] Ibid., 197–201.

[4] Ibid., 198.

[5] Ibid.

Gregersen recognizes that a response based on the understanding of evolution as a package deal offers no real comfort to creatures afflicted by suffering. A second theological step is needed to deal with the existential problem of evil, one that involves not only evolutionary theory and creation theology but also Christology and Pneumatology. In particular, Gregersen proposes, we need a theology of the cross, one that understands the cross from the perspective of a high Christology. He follows Richard Bauckham in seeing the New Testament as witnessing from the earliest times to a high Christology, in which Jesus is identified, implicitly or explicitly, with God's Word and Wisdom.[6] On the basis of this Christology, Gregersen insists that the truth of God is revealed in the cross of Jesus, in the experience of anguish, humiliation, pain, and death. The cross reveals God's true character: "If the cross of Christ belongs to God's eternal character (as the 'Lamb slain in eternity,' as is said in the Revelation of John), God's way of exercising sovereignty over all things in creation will also forever be characterized by God's self-giving nature."[7] Gregersen proposes, then, that God's kenotic self-giving, which finds such radical expression in the cross of Jesus, can also to be understood as characteristic of God as Creator: God's kenotic love is also expressed in the Creator giving creation its own active participation in creativity, which is symbolized in God's primordial blessing of the creaturely world. It is God's self-giving love that enables and embraces a world that evolves through its own creaturely dynamics.

What is the meaning of the self-giving of the cross for the creation in its suffering? Gregersen proposes that "the cross at once exemplifies and makes real that God bears the cost of

---

[6] Richard Bauckham, *God Crucified: Monotheism and Christology in the New Testament* (Grand Rapids, MI: William B. Eerdmans, 1998); *Jesus and the Eyewitnesses: The Gospels as Eyewitness Testimony* (Grand Rapids, MI: William B. Eerdmans, 2006).

[7] Gregersen, "The Cross of Christ in an Evolutionary World," 203.

suffering with the world."[8] The cross of Jesus is like a micro-cosm in which the suffering of the macrocosm is represented and lived out, and in which death and destruction are trans-formed in resurrection. In his ministry Jesus identifies with the outsider and the needy, acting against the law of selection and the need to compete, refusing to play the game of honor and shame. But he is rejected and abandoned, and is identified with the losers and the victims, even to the point of his crucifixion. This suggests a fundamental insight to Gregersen: "God the giver of life, who produced the package deal of natural order and disorder, is also the co-carrier of the costs of evolution."[9] In summarizing his view of deep incarnation, Gregersen writes:

> In this context, the incarnation of God in Christ can be understood as a radical or "deep" incarnation, that is, an incarnation into the very tissue of biological exis-tence and system of nature. Understood this way, the death of Christ becomes an icon of God's redemptive co-suffering with all sentient life as well as with the victims of social competition. God bears the costs of evolution, the price involved in the hardship of natural selection.[10]

What difference does this make to those who suffer? Certainly it makes a difference to the human sufferer to know that he or she is no longer alone. But Gregersen wants to say more than this. Because Jesus belongs eternally to God's identity, it is God who is present in the midst of creaturely suffering, and "wher-ever God is, God is not only passively enduring suffering, but is also in the process of actively transforming suffering."[11] God does not only suffer with creation but is so intimately

---

8 Ibid.
9 Ibid., 204.
10 Ibid., 205.
11 Ibid., 204.

involved with living creatures that "God's life-giving power spreads into the suffering and dying bodies of humans and animals." Redemption of these creatures does not depend on their subjective awareness, Gregersen says, but is "conditioned only by God's gracious power of sharing life with creatures."[12]

Elizabeth Johnson

Elizabeth Johnson has built on Gregersen's theology of deep incarnation several times, culminating in her *Ask the Beasts*, and more recently in *Creation and the Cross*.[13] She sees the incarnation as a new radical embodiment, in which the Wisdom/Word of God joins the material world to accomplish a new level of union between Creator and creature. She notes the axiom of the early church, "what is not assumed is not healed," which suggests that the incarnation brings salvation to all that is embraced by the Word made flesh. This has often been understood as referring particularly to all aspects of the humanity that are taken by the Word. Deep incarnation seeks to clarify a further extension of the impact of incarnation:

Deep incarnation extends this view to include all flesh. In the incarnation Jesus, the self-expressing Wisdom of God, conjoined the material conditions of all biological life forms (grasses and trees), and experienced the pain

---

[12] Ibid., 205.

[13] Elizabeth A. Johnson, "An Earthy Christology," *America: The National Catholic Review* 200, no. 12 (April 13, 2009): 27–30; "Deep Christology," in *From Logos to Christos: Essays in Christology in Honour of Joanne McWilliam*, ed. Ellen M. Leonard and Kate Merriman (Waterloo, ON: Wilfred Laurier University Press, 2009), 163–80; *Ask the Beasts: Darwin and the God of Love* (New York: Bloomsbury, 2014); "Jesus and the Cosmos: Soundings in Deep Ecology," in *Incarnation: On the Scope and Depth of Christology*, ed. Niels Gregersen (Minneapolis: Fortress, 2015), 133–56; *Creation and the Cross: The Mercy of God for a Planet in Peril* (Maryknoll, NY: Orbis Books, 2018).

common to all sensitive creatures (sparrows and seals). The flesh assumed in Jesus connects with all humanity, all biological life, all soil, the whole matrix of the material universe down to its very roots.[14]

The incarnation not only weds Jesus to humanity but also reaches beyond humanity to all living creatures and to the cosmic dust of which all earth creatures are composed. In this way, Johnson says, matter and flesh become part of God's own story forever.[15] The incarnation is a cosmic event.

Yet incarnation finds its expression in a specific concrete and local event—the life and ministry of Jesus of Nazareth that leads to his death and resurrection. Johnson reflects on Jesus's proclamation of the good news of the reign of God, and on his healing and liberating ministry. Although she recognizes that it would be anachronistic to attribute a contemporary ecological consciousness to Jesus, she points out that he inherited the creation faith of Israel, and that his proclamation of the nearness of the reign of God assumed that the natural world was included in the good news. His proclamation of this reign is filled with references to seeds, harvest, wheat, weeds, vineyards, fruit trees, rain, sunsets, sheep, and nesting birds. He speaks of God's providential care for lilies of the field and birds of the air. Jesus's healing practices and his meals show his understanding that the good news involves the whole of life. Along with Sallie McFague, Johnson speaks of all of this as the "christic paradigm" of God's "liberating, healing and inclusive love."[16] When we set this paradigm in the larger context of the evolving world, it can be argued that Jesus's ministry reveals that God's intent is fullness of life both for humanity, above all for poor human beings, but also for God's other living creatures.

---

[14] Johnson, *Ask the Beasts*, 196.

[15] Ibid., 197.

[16] Sallie McFague, *The Body of God* (Minneapolis: Fortress, 1993), 81.

The incarnation of the Word of God in matter and flesh leads ultimately to the death of Jesus on the cross. Reflecting on the radical self-emptying (*kenosis*) and self-humbling (Phil 2:7–8) involved in the Word of God becoming human, becoming like a slave, and accepting death on a cross, Johnson writes:

> This tremendous swoop from divine form to crucified human being traces an arc of divine humility. It credits the incomprehensible God with having a seemingly non-godly characteristic, especially when seen against the model of an omnipotent monarch, namely the ability to be self-emptying, self-limiting, self-offering, vulnerable, self-giving, in a word, creative Love in action.[17]

She sees the suffering and death of the Word incarnate as God's participation in pain and death from *within* the world of the flesh. With Pope Benedict she sees God as suffering with us in the Word made flesh.[18] With Gregersen, she sees the death of Christ as an icon of God's redemptive co-suffering with all sentient life. Johnson writes of the presence of the Spirit of the crucified Christ to suffering creatures: "Dwelling in the evolving world and acting in, with and under its natural processes, the Giver of life continuously knows and bears the cost of new life."[19] She asks whether this presence of God to suffering creatures makes any difference. Does it make a difference to a starving pelican chick? Her response is to say, with Christopher Southgate, that God's loving presence to creatures in their suffering is "one of the most significant things theology can say."[20] The indwelling, empowering Giver of Life, who

---

[17] Johnson, *Ask the Beasts*, 202.
[18] Benedict XVI, Homily at Aosta, July 24, 2009.
[19] Johnson, *Ask the Beasts*, 205.
[20] Ibid., 206.

companions all creatures in their individual lives, as well as in the whole process of their evolution, does not abandon the creature in its trial: "The cross gives warrant for locating the compassion of God right at the center of the affliction. The pelican chick does not die alone."[21]

Johnson proposes that a theology of deep incarnation also involves a theology of "deep resurrection." She sees Christ's resurrection as a promise of God, one that involves not only humanity, but also the whole creation. Christ is not only "first-born of the dead," but also "firstborn of all creation" (Col 1:15).[22] Johnson points to Paul Santmire's analysis of theological positions on this issue.[23] Some theologians, including Irenaeus, see all creatures as participating in the promised transformation. In this view, there is a symmetry between God creating all things and God saving all things. Others, including the great medieval theologians Aquinas and Bonaventure, and the Reformers Luther and Calvin, hold an asymmetrical view: Although God creates all creatures, God will not bring all to their own participation in final salvation.[24]

Johnson takes the symmetrical position. She argues that based on what we know of the character of God as self-giving love poured out on creation, we can trust that God not only sustains and cares about every sparrow (Mt 10:29; Lk 12:6), but that God will also bring each of them to redemptive fullness. She sees this position as based on the following core truths of faith and as coherent with their dynamism:

- The living God creates and cares for all creatures.
- This love encompasses all creatures even in their suffering and dying.

---

[21] Ibid. See also Johnson, *Creation and the Cross*, 187–89.

[22] Johnson, *Ask the Beasts*, 209.

[23] Paul Santmire, *The Travail of Nature: The Ambiguous Ecological Promise of Christian Theology* (Minneapolis: Fortress Press, 1985).

[24] Ibid., 228–29.

- These creatures are part of the flesh of the World which the Word of God joined via incarnation.
- The death and resurrection of Jesus offers hope of redemption for all flesh.
- The life-giving power of the Spirit who empowers all creation is also the power of resurrected life for all beings.[25]

Johnson insists, with theologians like Rahner, that we have no advance knowledge of life after death, even for humans. We have no clear concepts or imaginative picture of how God might accomplish the salvation of other creatures. Based on what we know of God, she says, we can assume that the redemptive fulfillment of each creature will be appropriate to each creature's capacities. This position is grounded only in Christian faith, in the revelation of the nature of the divine love found in Jesus Christ: "Given the personal presence of divine love to every creature in every moment, and the further revelation of the character of this love in the suffering and hope-filled story of Jesus Christ, there is warrant for holding that species and even individual creatures are not abandoned in death but taken into communion with the living God."[26] In a way we cannot imagine, the whole creation is to be transfigured in Christ.

Celia Deane-Drummond

Deep incarnation has been an important theme in Celia Deane-Drummond's theological work at the intersection of science and theology.[27] Deane-Drummond has consistently sought to show

---

[25] Johnson, *Ask the Beasts*, 231. See also *Creation and the Cross*, 189–94.

[26] Johnson, *Ask the Beasts*, 231.

[27] Celia Deane-Drummond, *Christ and Evolution: Wonder and Wisdom* (Minneapolis: Fortress, 2009). See her "Deep Incarnation and Ecojustice as Theodrama," in *Ecological Awareness: Exploring Religion, Eth-*

that the incarnation of God in Jesus Christ has significance for the whole universe of creatures and not just for human beings. Like others involved in the theology of deep incarnation, she has explored an understanding of Christ as divine Wisdom. What is distinctive to her approach is that she has sought to develop deep incarnation by using the concept of theo-drama, drawing on the work of Hans Urs von Balthasar. She sees theo-drama as a better starting point for deep incarnation than either ontological or historical approaches to Christology.

One reason for Deane-Drummond's attraction to von Balthasar's theo-drama is that it is oriented toward the experiential and the existential. She also finds a cosmic dimension to his thought in his appropriation of Patristic writers, particularly Maximus the Confessor. Although she recognizes that von Balthasar does not himself extend Christ's incarnation to the wider creation, as she seeks to do in her own ecological theology, Deane-Drummond nevertheless finds his dramatic approach to Christology fruitful for a theology of deep incarnation.

However, she approaches von Balthasar's theology in a critical way, differing from him in his punitive approach to the cross of Jesus, and in his view of God as directing the whole drama of the cross. In her own theology, she seeks to leave room for God to act through improvisation.[28] Her theology is also more inclusive of human agency, and far more involving of God's other creatures in salvation. She differs from von Balthasar in grounding her theology in the evolutionary and

---

ics and Aesthetics, ed. Sigurd Bergmann and Heather Eaton (Berlin: LIT, 2011), 193–206; "Who on Earth Is Jesus Christ? Plumbing the Depths of Deep Incarnation," in *Christian Faith and the Earth: Current Paths and Emerging Horizons in Ecotheology*, ed. Ernst M. Conradie et al. (London: Bloomsbury T. & T. Clark, 2014), 31–50; "The Wisdom of Fools? A Theo-Dramatic Interpretation of Deep Incarnation," in *Incarnation: On the Scope and Depth of Christology*, ed. Gregersen, 177–202; *A Primer in Ecotheology: Theology for a Fragile Earth* (Eugene, OR: Cascade Books, 2017).

[28] Deane-Drummond, "The Wisdom of Fools?" 188, 191.

ecological sciences, and in giving a greater role to the Holy Spirit in the Christological theo-drama.

Granted these critical positions, Deane-Drummond finds the approach to Christ through drama appropriate both scientifically and theologically. In terms of science she sees a dramatic theology as fitting with the great drama of evolutionary emergence. In terms of theology she finds it able to bring out the particular way in which the Word is embedded in the frail, bodily, and mortal event of Jesus, and above all in his death on the cross. Drama is well suited to bring out the specific action of God in contingent events such as the cross. A theo-dramatic approach, she says, can avoid the inevitability and the fatalism of grand narratives. At the same time, von Balthasar's theo-dramatic approach suggests the fundamental role played by the subject who contemplates the cross of Jesus. It does not claim a complete, and false, objectivity. It suggests, rather, a contemplative or mystical engagement with, and participation in, the event.

Deane-Drummond is sympathetic to von Balthasar's way of understanding the cross as the revelation of the dynamic self-giving love that is at the heart of the Trinity. The drama of the cross in our history points to the drama of the self-emptying of the Father's heart in the generation of the Son. It is this self-giving love of the divine triune life that is at work in the whole drama of creation and salvation:

> From the beginning of creation, through to the incarnation and consummation, the Trinitarian movement is the dramatic movement of God's love and grace in the world. Creation, then, is not so much a backdrop against which human history is played out, but the *first act in the overall drama*, that eventually comes to expression in the incarnation of the Word (or Wisdom) made Flesh.[29]

---

[29] Deane-Drummond, *A Primer in Ecotheology*, 84–85.

Von Balthasar's theo-drama famously involves his reflection on Holy Saturday, when Christ enters into the place of the dead, and into the human fear of death, in order to bring forgiveness, liberation, and hope. Deane-Drummond extends this thought to include suffering and dying creation. She sees Christ as entering deep into the place not only of human suffering but also of ecological and climatic catastrophe. Christians are called to follow Christ to this place and to act in the Spirit for the healing of the creation. In the light of Christ's resurrection, Deane-Drummond argues, the concept of theo-drama can be extended so that Christ's death and resurrection are seen as fully inclusive in scope, "widening out to the universal reach of God's love shown in Christ to all creatures."[30]

For von Balthasar absolute beauty is revealed in the cross. Despite its terrible ugliness by ordinary reckoning, it nevertheless becomes the supreme icon of beauty because it is the revelation of God's passionate love. If Christ is the form of beauty, Deane-Drummond suggests, then we are challenged to appreciate "not just those forms of creation that seem most appealing to us, but also those creatures that seem to us in aesthetic terms to be repellent or even repugnant."[31] Von Balthasar's view of the world in tragic terms, Deane-Drummond proposes, can be extended so "that we can see this tragedy as rippling out into the fabric of creation, in much the same way that the Logos of Christ is also echoed in the cosmos as a whole."[32]

Deep incarnation, for Deane-Drummond, then, is best seen as "the *transformative and dramatic movement* of God in Christ."[33] Although Christ takes central place in the theo-drama, this transformative action can only be understood in terms of the active presence of the Holy Spirit. Deep incarna-

---

[30] Deane-Drummond, "The Wisdom of Fools?" 200–201.

[31] Deane-Drummond, *Christ and Evolution*, 143.

[32] Ibid.

[33] Deane-Drummond, *A Primer in Ecotheology*, 87.

tion also necessarily involves a deep Pneumatology, with the Spirit at work in the space between creation and its re-creation in glory. Deane-Drummond sees the place of the Spirit as fundamental to ecological theology, because the Spirit is the space of human participation in the drama alongside Christ, acting in solidarity with suffering humanity, and the suffering creatures "whose extinctions are littered all around us."[34] In this space, the Spirit calls human beings to ecological conversion and to an ecological ethics: "If we are to follow deep incarnation to its limits, then it must be associated with an ethical demand to take an active part in the shared drama, a common history of the earth, and therefore love God and neighbour, acting with sensitivity and responsibly towards the earth and its creatures."[35]

Christopher Southgate

Christopher Southgate has devoted a great deal of his academic work to offering a theological response to the suffering of creatures in an evolutionary world. One of his key contributions is his proposal that a theological response to the suffering that is built into an evolutionary world requires a "compound evolutionary theodicy." He outlines this theodicy in his 2008 monograph, *The Groaning of Creation*, and develops it in a 2014 essay.[36] He seeks to respond to the fact that, for the human observer, the evolutionary world appears to be deeply

---

[34] Ibid.

[35] Deane-Drummond, "The Wisdom of Fools," 201.

[36] Christopher Southgate, *The Groaning of Creation: God, Evolution and the Problem of Evil* (Louisville, KY: Westminster John Knox Press, 2008); "Does God's Care Make Any Difference? Theological Reflections on the Suffering of God's Creatures," in *Christian Faith and the Earth,* ed. Conradie, 97–114. My own reflections here and later in this book build on my article "Christopher Southgate's Compound Theodicy: Parallel Searchings," *Zygon* 53, no. 3 (September 2018): 680–90.

ambiguous, marked not only by values such as cooperation, fruitfulness, and beauty but also by disvalues such as cruelty, loss, and extinction. What is beautiful emerges only through evolutionary processes that involve predation, competition for resources, pain, and death.

Southgate points out that the traditional Christian solution to the problem of evil, in which the disvalues of the natural world are said to be due to human sin, no longer works: "We can be clear now that this is simply an understandable pre-scientific anachronism—yes, it is true that modern humans have been devastators of their environment and precipitators of many extinctions, but we also know that processes of predation and disease, and other much larger extinction events than the ones yet caused by humans, long preceded the evolution of humankind."[37] If human sin is not the cause of the pain and loss in nature, this seems to leave the responsibility with God. How can we speak with integrity of a God of love in relation to the suffering built into God's creation? Southgate responds to this question with his articulation of the four interrelated components that make up his compound theodicy.

The first component is Southgate's *only way* argument. He sees God as limited or constrained in achieving God's loving purposes in creating a universe of creatures, because God is working with creaturely reality that is limited in its possibilities. Southgate's best guess is that there are logical limitations to God's creation of a life-bearing universe: it is not logically possible for God to create the kind of world we inhabit without the costs that come with evolution. Southgate writes: "A world of competition and natural selection was the only way God could give rise to creaturely values of the sort we know to have evolved in the biosphere of Earth."[38] But he also insists that more than this *only way* argument is required

---

[37] Southgate, "Does God's Care Make Any Difference?" 100.

[38] Ibid., 101.

if theology is to respond theologically to the pain and loss of individual creatures—three further components are needed for his theodicy.

The second component is that Southgate understands *God as co-suffering* with all creatures. He strongly embraces the theological tradition of God's presence to each creature. God is present to creatures both in their flourishing and their suffering, and no creature suffers or dies alone. He takes up Gregersen's theology of deep incarnation, agreeing with him that the cross of Christ expresses God's loving solidarity with all creatures, particularly with the victims of evolution.[39] Southgate proposes that the cross of Christ reveals a God who suffers with all suffering creatures, and that this suffering of God with creatures makes a difference, "at some deep existential level" both to God and to the creature. Not only is the creature not alone in moments of suffering, but also the creature, "in whatever sense, knows this, and that this awareness makes a difference."[40]

The third component of Southgate's theodicy, based on the Christian conviction of the resurrection of Christ and its meaning for the whole creation, is the hope that suffering creatures will participate in God's *eschatological fulfillment*. Picking up Jay McDaniel's phrase, Southgate suggest that the pelican chick that has been pushed out of the nest may come to experience "pelican heaven": "If we take altogether seriously the loving character and purposes of God, I think we cannot believe that lives consisting of nothing but suffering are the end for those creatures that experience them."[41] This line of thought leads him to the conviction that our

---

[39] See Southgate, *The Groaning of Creation*, 76–77; "Does God's Care Make Any Difference?" 103.

[40] Southgate, "Does God's Care Make Any Difference?" 112.

[41] Ibid.; *The Groaning of Creation*, 78–91.

eschatological fulfillment, or our heaven, will be "rich in creaturely diversity."[42]

The last component in Southgate's compound theodicy is his idea of the high calling of redeemed humanity to be *co-redeemers with God* in the drawing together of all things. Christians, who understand themselves as made in the image of God the Trinity are called to participate in the Trinity's longing for, and work toward, a peaceful, holy, and loving creation. Christians, then, will delight in systems that manifest cooperation and self-transcendence, such as those found in tropical forests, in symbiosis in the oceans, and in the lives of social animals. Sharing in God's longing for creaturely cooperation, he says, humans are called to be active agents, not only cooperating with God in enabling the natural world to flourish, but also participating in its eschatological fulfillment. Later in this book I take up Southgate's fourfold structure, with some differences of expression and emphasis.

Richard Bauckham

In his discussion of deep incarnation, Richard Bauckham begins by distinguishing different forms of divine presence.[43] There is not only the metaphysical presence of the Creator to each creature, enabling its existence, but also the personal and free presence of God with and in creatures. Alongside God's universal creative presence, God can also make God's self present in creation in the freedom of love. God's presence, then, is not simply universal, but also historical and particular. Bauckham points to the many different forms of divine presence found in the Bible and the Christian tradition: "They include theophany, vision, encounter, word of address, conversation,

---

[42] Southgate, "Does God's Care Make Any Difference?" 113.

[43] Richard Bauckham, "The Incarnation and the Cosmic Christ," in *Incarnation: On the Scope and Depth of Christology*, ed. Gregersen, 25–56.

inspiration, empowerment, providential care, and sacrament, as well as incarnation."[44]

Bauckham strongly resists collapsing all forms of divine presence into the incarnation. He insists on the uniqueness of incarnation, in part through his emphatic use of prepositions: in the incarnation, God is not simply present *in* or *with* a creature, but is present *as* the particular human Jesus of Nazareth. Bauckham opposes some modern theologies, such as that of John Macquarrie, in which God's presence in Jesus is understood as differing from God's presence in other creatures only in degree. For Bauckham, God's presence in the incarnation is different in *kind* to other forms of divine presence to creatures.

Building on his earlier work on Christology, Bauckham rejects the idea that the New Testament represents a low Christology (emphasizing Christ's humanity) that only later develops into a high Christology (emphasizing Christ's divinity).[45] In his view of the New Testament, Jesus is distinguished from the beginning by the unique function he fulfills on behalf of God, as Messiah, Savior, Lord, and as the one who sits at the right hand of God on the throne of the universe. He points out that in the Jewish world, these functions belong to the divine identity. A close study of the New Testament reveals that worship of Jesus by Jewish Christians was not a late development. From the beginning, the first Jewish Christians saw Jesus as participating in the unique divine identity of the one God of Israel. Based on this "Christology of divine identity," Bauckham defends a high Christology in which the incarnation of God in Jesus is understood as distinct in kind from other forms of divine presence.

---

[44] Ibid., 27.

[45] Richard Bauckham, *Jesus and the God of Israel: God Crucified and Other Studies of the New Testament Theology of Divine Identity* (Grand Rapids, MI: William B. Eerdmans, 2009); *Jesus and the Eyewitnesses: The Gospels as Eyewitness Testimony* (Grand Rapids, MI: William B. Eerdmans, 2006).

He sees this unique presence of God in the incarnation as salvific because it is the personal and intentional presence of God, in an act of loving identification with all humanity. God identifies God's self *as* a worldly reality, Jesus of Nazareth, in order to be *with* all other human beings. From his baptism to the cross, Jesus practices self-identifying love for others, reaching out to the most abandoned, even to the degradation of his death, and so brings the love of God into the lives of others. Through his resurrection, and in the Spirit, Jesus's loving identification for others is universalized and becomes available to all. The saving effect of incarnation affects humanity, not by an automatic or quasi-physical process, but in a fully personal way by relationship with Jesus.

What of the wider creation? How is it related to the incarnation? Bauckham sees the Bible as witnessing to a redemption in Christ that involves the renewal of the whole creation through participation in the eternal life of God (in texts such as Col 1:15–20; Eph 1:9–10; 1 Cor 8:6; Heb 1:2–3; Rev 3:14). How are we to understand the cosmic role of the Word made flesh? Since the Bible sees all things as created in the cosmic Word, Bauckham rejects the idea that the incarnation is to be understood as the entry of the Word into a creation where the Word had previously been absent. At the same time he rejects the opposite idea that the incarnation is simply a more concentrated form of already existing presence, insisting: "It is a new kind of presence."[46]

How does this new kind of presence make a difference to the creation? Bauckham discusses the traditional idea of Jesus as microcosm of the whole creation (Maximus the Confessor and Bonaventure) and contemporary emergence theory (Arthur Peacocke and Jacob Klapwijk). He judges them both to be inadequate models for deep incarnation because, in terms of modern science, humans can no longer be thought

---

[46] Bauckham, "The Incarnation and the Cosmic Christ," 36.

of as somehow summing up all other creatures. He is also critical of Teilhard de Chardin's view of the progressive directionality of evolution and does not think that the new creation can be seen simply as the outcome of evolutionary processes: "However, new creation is far too radical a novelty to be seen as one more emergent novelty in the immanent process of the universe. It is a novelty that, by definition, is comparable only with the novelty of *creatio ex nihilo*."[47]

Bauckham understands deep incarnation in a more ecological perspective, in which humans are interrelated with all other species and with inanimate nature in an interdependent web of life. He seeks a theology that can avoid anthropocentrism, and support the integrity of other species and of other aspects of the natural world. He sees the goal of the whole creation as coming about through the incarnation, in a relational act, a gracious act of divine self-giving love:

> It comes about through Jesus Christ's loving presence in and with the whole creation, which is a unique form of divine and human engagement with the ecological interrelatedness of all things. It proves transformative for the whole creation because the loving self-identification of the crucified Christ with the whole creation in the tragedy of its disharmony and decay as well as the glory of its profusion and vitality draws the whole creation with him into the eschatological novelty of his resurrection.[48]

In the incarnation, God is freely present within the ecological relatedness of all things. In his life and ministry Jesus of Nazareth participates in the interrelatedness with the wider creation that all humans have. But in the divine intention, and through the resurrection, this interrelatedness is universalized.

---

47 Ibid., 54.
48 Ibid., 55.

In the risen Christ, the human particularity of Jesus is united with the divine capacity to be universally present.

Bauckham identifies with Bonaventure's view of Christ as the mediating center of creation: Christ "is the ecological center of all creation, enabling all things, in their interconnectedness, to find their unity and wholeness in relationship to God."[49] The risen Christ, firstborn of the new creation, is also the goal of creation. For Bauckham, then, the Word of God is not incarnate in all reality, but transforms the whole of reality: "Through his unique self-engagement with the world *as* the human being Jesus, God will be present *with* and *in* all things, finally without reservation or impediment, transfiguring all with glory."[50]

Gregersen: Refinements and Developments of Deep Incarnation

Niels Henrik Gregersen's thought on deep incarnation has continued to develop, partly in his engagement with other theologians at the international symposium on deep incarnation held at Elsinore in 2011, and then in his J. K. Russell lectures at the Center for Theology and the Natural Sciences, Berkeley, in 2013.[51] In what follows I attempt to encapsulate some key refinements and developments in Gregersen's

---

[49] Ibid., 57.

[50] Ibid., 55.

[51] For the Elsinore symposium see Gregersen, *Incarnation: On the Scope and Depth of Christology*. For the J. K Russell lectures and responses, see *Theology & Science* 11:4 (2013): 370–468. See also his "The Extended Body: the Social Body of Jesus according to Luke," *Dialog: A Journal of Theology* 51:3 (2012): 235–45; "The Idea of Deep Incarnation: Biblical and Patristic Resources," in *To Discern Creation in a Scattering World*, ed. F. Depoortere and J. Haers (Leuven: Peters, 2013), 319–41; "The Emotional Christ: Bonaventure and Deep Incarnation," *Dialog: A Journal of Theology* 55:3 (2016): 247–61.

thought on deep incarnation. In several of his later articles Gregersen offers a careful description of what he means by deep incarnation:

> "Deep Incarnation" is the view that God's own Logos (Wisdom and Word) was made flesh in Jesus the Christ in such a comprehensive manner that God, by assuming the particular life story of Jesus the Jew from Nazareth, also conjoined the material conditions of creaturely existence ("all flesh"), shared and ennobled the fate of all biological life forms ("grass" and "lilies"), and experienced the pain of sensitive creatures ("sparrows" and "foxes") from within. Deep incarnation thus presupposes a radical embodiment that reaches into the roots (*radices*) of material and biological existence as well as into the darker sides of creation: the *tenebrae creationis*.[52]

In order to speak of the uniqueness of God's presence in the incarnate Christ, Gregersen takes up Bauckham's use of prepositions, to distinguish between the unique presence of God in the incarnation and all other forms of divine presence. Noting that Bauckham's "identity Christology" had been formative for his original development of the concept of deep incarnation, Gregersen says that in God's loving self-identification *as* Jesus, God is identified *with* and *for* all people, and *with* and *for* the larger community of creation.[53] It is not appropriate, then, to say simply that God is incarnate in all that is, or to say with Mark Johnson that "the incarnation of the divine is ubiquitous."[54]

---

[52] Gregersen, "The Extended Body of Christ," 225–26.

[53] Gregersen, "Deep Incarnation: Opportunities and Challenges" in Gregersen, *Incarnation: On the Scope and Depth of Christology*, 363–64.

[54] Mark Johnson, *Saving God* (Princeton, NJ: Princeton University Press, 2009), 121.

Gregersen speaks of three senses of incarnation. *Strict sense* incarnation applies to Jesus Christ, in his lifetime, in the church as the body of Christ, and in his cosmic role. *Broad sense* incarnation points to Jesus Christ as "sharing the depth and scope of social and geo-biological conditions of the entire cosmos."[55] Gregersen adds a third sense of incarnation, in which strict sense and broad sense are united in what he calls the *soteriological* sense of the incarnation, in which Christ "co-suffers with and for all suffering creatures" and works for their salvation through the life-giving power of the Holy Spirit.[56]

Gregersen promotes a concept of the extended body of Christ. In ordinary Christian language we commonly speak of the body of Christ in Jesus's historical life and ministry, in his post-resurrection exalted body, and in the social body of Christ that is the church. To these Gregersen adds the idea of the whole creation as the cosmic body of Christ, pointing to Paul's letter to the Romans where there is a deep connection between the church as the body of Christ and the liberation of the whole creation (Rom 8:18–23), and to Colossians and Ephesians where the whole creation is reconciled in the risen Christ, in a theology of the cosmic Christ (Col 1:15–20, 2:9; Eph 2:11–22).

Gregersen makes it clear that he sees deep incarnation as a fully trinitarian theology. He speaks of the "stretch" of the Trinity, of the relation between the Father and the Word, which is bridged by the Spirit.[57] It is this "divine stretch" between the Father and the eternal Word, mediated by the Spirit, which is the presupposition of the divine stretch, or reach, into the depths of creation in deep incarnation. Deep incarnation is mediated by the Holy Spirit of God at every point.

---

[55] Gregersen, "*Cur deus caro*: Jesus and the Cosmic Story," *Theology and Science* 11, no. 4 (2013): 370–93, at 385.

[56] Ibid., 386.

[57] See, for example, Gregersen, "The Extended Body of Christ," 235.

For Gregersen there is no sharp distinction between the person of Christ and the saving work of Christ, and no need for an elaborate theory of atonement, because the presence of the incarnate Word is itself saving.[58] Salvation is the communion between God and creatures brought about through the Word and in the Spirit. What theology must do today, in Gregersen's view, is to show how God's presence as Jesus is already saving for the whole creation: "Salvation means being embraced by God's self-embodying Logos/Wisdom who is interweaved with the complex material-spiritual world for the sake of its transformation."[59]

Along with Elizabeth Johnson, Gregersen proposes a concept of deep suffering and resurrection, whereby, in Christ, God enters into the pain of all creatures, and is for and with them in radical love, bringing them salvation.[60] It is the risen Christ, in his "extended" or "comprehensive" body, who co-suffers with all creatures.[61] Gregersen acknowledges that from our limited, temporal framework, we can say only that the Logos/Wisdom was always meant to become incarnate in Jesus. From the perspective of the eternal divine life, however, he says that there never was, and never will be, a disembodied Logos. Logos was always embodied, and will always be embodied: "Accordingly, there never was or will be a divine life without Christ knowing suffering and death from within. As stated in the Revelation to John, the Lamb is 'slain from the foundation of the world' (Rev. 13:8)."[62]

Gregersen insists that the "Logos/Son of God contained not just the niceties of the cosmic order but also the nastiness

---

[58] Gregersen, "The Emotional Christ: Bonaventure and Deep Incarnation," 254.

[59] Gregersen, "Deep Incarnation: Opportunities and Challenges," 368.

[60] Gregersen, "Deep Incarnation and Kenosis: In, With and As: A Response to Ted Peters," *Dialog: A Journal of Theology* 52, no. 3 (2013): 251–62, at 260.

[61] Gregersen, "The Extended Body of Christ," 249.

[62] Gregersen, "Deep Incarnation: Opportunities and Challenges," 370.

of ugliness, pain, and death, in as well as outside of Galilee."[63] He sees the resurrection as "impinging on every moment and epoch in history, and as close to every place in the vast cosmic space."[64] Gregersen argues that today we need to go beyond Paul's "apocalyptic" view of the temporal sequence of cross, resurrection of Jesus, church, resurrection of the faithful, and liberation of creation.[65] Already in the later Pauline writings the resurrection of the faithful can be spoken of in the present tense. Incarnation and resurrection are seen as something "enduring or processual."[66] The reconciliation and redemption of all things are a "still-deeper growth into the body of Christ, who is the deep coinherence of everything that exists: 'In him all things hold together' (Col. 1:17)."[67]

Gregersen's strong view of God's universal presence to creatures does not diminish his focus on the suffering and loss that is part of an evolutionary world. He does not think that all natural and human events reveal God, or reveal God in the same way:

> Neither divine omnipresence nor incarnation presuppose that God is "omni-manifest," that is, revealed in all the vicissitudes of natural evolution and human history, including natural and human horrors. Rather, the point is that the embodied Word of God shares *from within* the sufferings of all who suffer from the powers of tsunamis, earthquakes and hunger, and *takes the side of* the victims of the horrors that human beings inflict upon one another.[68]

---

[63] Gregersen, "The Extended Body of Christ," 248.

[64] Ibid., 250.

[65] Ibid., 243, 248. See also Gregersen's "Deep Incarnation: Opportunities and Challenges," 365, 369–70.

[66] Gregersen, "The Extended Body of Christ," 244.

[67] Ibid.

[68] Ibid., 235.

Although God is not revealed in the horrors that befall people, and other creatures, God is not absent from suffering creatures, but is radically present with them and for them, as compassionate love and as promise. So God is lovingly present to all things, but not everything in nature reveals God, or reveals God fully: "The ruthless hardship of natural selection is part of God's creativity, but does not reveal the nature of God."[69]

In recent work, Gregersen has reflected on the relationship between deep incarnation and the thought of Bonaventure, particularly his concept of Christ as the microcosm of the whole creation. He refers to one of Bonaventure's sermons, in which he speaks of Christ as a human who is sharing being with all creatures: "Indeed, he possesses being with rocks, lives among the plants, senses with animals, and understands with angels. Since Christ, as a human being, has something from all of creation, and was transfigured, all is said to be transfigured in him."[70]

Gregersen acknowledges Bauckham's critique of the microcosm approach and his preference for a more ecological and relational model of the relationship between Christ and the rest of creation. But Gregersen fears a merely external relationality and seeks an internal relationality, where "the cosmic relations are co-constitutive of Christ."[71] In Gregersen's proposal of internal relationality, "The incarnate Christ cannot at all be the incarnate Logos, unless he is internally related to the cosmos at large."[72] Science now tells us that we are all made of the same stuff as the stars. We all spring from Matter-Energy, endowed with Information. Evolutionary genetics tells us that

---

[69] Gregersen, "*Cur deus caro*: Jesus and the Cosmic Story," 386.

[70] Bonaventure, *Sermones dominicales* 9.12, trans. Timothy T. Johnson, *The Sunday Sermons of St. Bonaventure* (New York: Franciscan Institute Publications, 2008), 217. See Gregersen, "*Cur deus caro*: Jesus and the Cosmic Story," 387.

[71] Gregersen, "*Cur deus caro*: Jesus and the Cosmic Story," 387.

[72] Ibid.

we creatures of earth belong to the same ecological community and share a deep history. We can no longer think of ourselves simply as individuals whose reality ends with our skins. Gregersen insists that the body of Christ cannot be genuinely incarnate "apart from the entire nexus of the world of Energy, Matter and Information."[73] Christ is not merely relating with men and women, sparrows and foxes, but is also sharing the basic creaturely conditions with them.

In Gregersen's judgment, Bonaventure's concept of Christ as the microcosm of creation can have new meaning in today's context. He sees Bonaventure's theology as "a distinct medieval version of central motifs of deep incarnation."[74] For Bonaventure the Wisdom of God, made flesh for the redemption of the world, is also the exemplary principle for the creation of the whole universe. For both Bonaventure and for Gregersen's concept of deep incarnation, the particularity of Christ is universal in meaning and in its effect.

Gregersen points to two ways in which he sees deep incarnation as differing from Bonaventure: (1) deep incarnation sees the Word of God as embracing the chaotic, messy, painful, and even sinful, aspects of creation in a way that Bonaventure does not; (2) in deep incarnation it is God in God's self who is conjoined with suffering creation in the cross of Christ, while Bonaventure limits the suffering of Christ to his human nature. Following Martin Luther, Gregersen attributes the compassion, humility, and suffering of the cross not simply to the human nature, but to the single divine-human subject, and therefore to God. This enables Gregersen to see God as radically identifying with the world of creation, in all its complexity and contingency, in order to transform it from within.

Nevertheless, Gregersen thinks that the Franciscan theology of Bonaventure, with its emphasis on the humble Christ

---

[73] Ibid.

[74] Gregersen, "The Emotional Christ: Bonaventure and Deep Incarnation," 254.

of crib and cross, and its concept of the microcosm, has internal resources for expressing the full implications of the self-humbling of divine Wisdom into the material world. What Gregersen wants to add to Bonaventure is that "Christ is not only a microcosm of the ordered and harmonious cosmos, but also shares, in his humble story from crib to cross, the fragile conditions of physical, biological and mental creatures."[75] In addition to these insights from Bonaventure, Gregersen points to the later Franciscan view of Scotus, who makes it clear that the divine Word was eternally predestined to come to the world of creation. In this Franciscan view, incarnation is not solely about human sin, but is also "about the overall unification of love between Creator and creature."[76] As Gregersen has brought deep incarnation into dialogue with Bonaventure's thought, I will seek, in the next three chapters, to bring it into dialogue with the thought of three other great theologians of incarnation: Irenaeus, Athanasius, and Karl Rahner.

---

[75] Ibid.
[76] Ibid.

2

Irenaeus and the Earthly Incarnation of the Word

In this chapter, I explore ways in which the theology of Irenaeus (c. 130–198) can be thought of as a foundation for, and to some extent a forerunner of, contemporary theologies of deep incarnation.[1] Irenaeus came to Rome from Smyrna in Asia Minor (Izmir, in today's Turkey) in the middle of the second century. He tells of being profoundly influenced in his early life by Polycarp, who had known John, the disciple of Jesus. He became a leading figure in the churches of Lyons and Vienne. His *Against Heresies* and his shorter *The Demonstration of the Apostolic Preaching* respond to the teachings of Marcion and Valentinus, both of whom had led house churches in Rome, before later distancing themselves from the wider Christian community.[2]

---

[1] In this chapter, and those following on Athanasius and Rahner, I am building on some relevant sections of my *Christian Understandings of Creation: The Historical Trajectory* (Minneapolis: Fortress Press, 2017).

[2] *Against Heresies* (hereafter *AH*) can be found in the *Source chétiennes* series, 263–64, 293–94, 210–11, 100, 152–53 (Paris: *Les éditions du Cerf*, 1952–82), and *The Demonstration of the Apostolic Preaching* (hereafter *Demonstration*) in *Source chétiennes*, 406 (Paris: *Les éditions du Cerf*, 1995). English translation of the first three books of *AH* is from the Ancient Christian Writers series (New York: Newman): book 1, vol. 55 (1992), and book 2, vol. 64 (2012), both trans. Dominic J. Unger,

In Marcion's thought, the creator God of the Hebrew Scriptures is seen as an inferior judgmental God, the Demiurge, who is completely other than the loving Father proclaimed by Jesus Christ. In the far more complex Valentinian position, often called Gnostic, the creator of the world is a lowly and unhappy exile from the divine realm of the Pleroma (fullness). This divine realm is made of thirty Aeons, a descending hierarchy of emanations from the supreme principle, the Father, who is also called "Depth" (*Bythos*). Matter and flesh arise as ignoble and squalid side effects from the disastrous jealousy and discord among the Aeons that make up the Pleroma. In this Valentinian position, as Irenaeus says, the material creation takes its beginning "from ignorance and grief, fear and bewilderment."[3] In stark contrast, Irenaeus defends the goodness of the one God of creation and salvation, the beauty and goodness of the creation, and the earthly reality of the flesh of the Savior.

The One Down-to-Earth Economy of Creation and Salvation

Irenaeus insists that there is only one God, who is both the Father of Jesus Christ and "the Creator God who made heaven and earth and all things in them."[4] Speaking of this God, Irenaeus writes: "There is nothing either above him or after him, and he was influenced by no one but, rather, made all things

---

revised John J. Dillon; book 3, vol. 65 (2012) trans. Dominic J. Unger, rev. Irenaeus M. C. Steenberg. Translation of books 4 and 5 is from the Anti-Nicene Fathers series, vol. 1 (Edinburgh, 1887; reprinted Grand Rapids, MI: Eerdmans, 2012), trans. A. Roberts and W. J. Rambaut. I will slightly modify the translations by substituting "the human" or "human being" for the generic "man." English translation of the *Demonstration* is from John Behr, *St. Irenaeus of Lyons. On the Apostolic Preaching* (Crestwood, NY: St. Vladimir's Seminary Press, 1997).

[3] *AH* 1.2.3.
[4] *AH* 2.1.1.

by his own counsel and free will, since he alone is God, and he alone is Lord, and he alone is Creator, and he alone is Father, and he alone contains all things, and he himself gives existence to all things."[5] The full identity between this one and only transcendent God of creation and the God of Jesus Christ is a central plank in Irenaeus's opposition to the views of both Marcion and Valentinus.

As Denis Minns points out, Irenaeus's religious awe and love for the Creator goes hand in hand with his religious awe and love for the good world that this God creates. Irenaeus is amazed that anyone could think that a weak, jealous God, or anything less than God, could have brought into being such an abundant and beautiful world.[6] He has no sympathy for a negative view of the created world: "He takes it for granted that the created world, in all its rich diversity, is a place of wonder and delight, and deduces that it has been created by a God of infinitely rich diversity and goodness whose purpose is that his sentient creatures should endure forever, always discovering new occasions for wonder and delight in God."[7] Creation is the work of love, a generous, endlessly bountiful love, and not the work of a petty, envious, and small-minded creator.[8]

It is Jesus Christ, the Word made flesh, and above all his cross, that reveal the true nature of the love from which creation springs. John Behr points out that, for Irenaeus, "the Cross is the definitive event in the revelation of God, occuring within our history yet with a significance that is eternal; the only perspective from which one can speak of the Word of God is that of the Cross."[9] From the perspective of the

---

[5] Ibid.

[6] Denis Minns, *Irenaeus: An Introduction* (London: T&T Clark, 2010), 33. See *AH* 2.2.1; 4.3; 10.3; 25.2; 26.3; 29.2; 30.3; 3.praef.

[7] Minns, *Irenaeus: An Introduction*, 33–34.

[8] *AH* 3.praef.

[9] John Behr, *Irenaeus of Lyons: Identifying Christianity* (Oxford: Oxford University Press, 2013), 134.

cross, Irenaeus sees the one great economy of God as eternally embracing both creation and salvation. He uses the term *economy* in a truly universal sense, bringing together all that God does for God's creatures.[10] As Behr notes, there are times when Irenaeus views the economy synchronically, as when he presents the whole Bible, in all its different parts, as constituting a portrait of Jesus Christ, like a beautiful mosaic of a king.[11] At other times he discusses the one economy diachronically and developmentally, and he speaks of the two Hands of God, the Word and the Spirit, gradually fashioning the salvation of creatures throughout history.

The incarnation is central to everything for Irenaeus. M. C. Steenberg writes that this centering on the incarnation, and looking back to creation from the perspective of the incarnation, leads Irenaeus to three foundational convictions about creation.[12] First, he sees God as creating out of sheer love, from the divine goodness, so that the matter and flesh of creation are the self-expression of divine goodness.[13] Second, he insists that God creates ex nihilo. God has no need of intermediaries, such as angels, or any form of lesser deity, but creates all entities in the universe directly.[14] Third, he sees the whole creation as directed to the Word made flesh, and in this Word to its eschatological future, when creation is to be renewed and the human being will be fully in the image and likeness of Christ.[15] In Irenaeus's Christocentric picture, the beginning involves the end, which is the incarnate Christ and the transformation of all things in him, and the end informs the beginning.

---

[10] Ibid., 125. Of course, Irenaeus like other theologians can also speak of particular moments and acts of God as economies.

[11] Ibid. and *AH* 1.8.10.

[12] M. C. Steenberg, *Irenaeus on Creation: The Cosmic Christ and the Saga of Redemption* (Leiden and Boston: Brill, 2008), 29–60.

[13] *AH* 3.25.5.

[14] *AH* 2.10.2; 2.28.7; *Demonstration*, 4.

[15] *AH* 5.25–35.

It is the divine love, fully revealed only in Christ and his cross, which radically unites creation and the saving incarnation in one economy. For Irenaeus creation and incarnation are two parts of the one overarching act of God. His concept of the one economy of God can be considered a theology of history, which is based on the conviction that God wants human beings to grow into a community in union with God by gradual stages, and that God enables this development in a loving, patient, and noncoercive manner.[16] The Word becomes incarnate, Irenaeus says, to "accustom humankind to receive God, and accustom God to dwell in humanity."[17] Unlike contemporary deep incarnation's attempt to engage with the breadth of the whole creation, Irenaeus's focus in his incarnational theology is often on the human, and he can speak of the wider creation as made for the benefit of the human.[18] He has, however, a positive view of the wider creation, seeing the human as always implanted in this world of matter and flesh. As I will explore later, he has a theology of recapitulation in Christ that involves "all things," and a theology of eschatological salvation that includes the whole creation.

Adam plays a central role in Irenaeus's reflections on the economy. Against the gnostic tendency to exalt the spiritual at the expense of the body, Irenaeus takes every opportunity to remind his readers that the human being is made from mud. Of course, Adam and Eve are not simply individuals for Irenaeus, but symbolize the whole of humanity, since all humans come from them. Minns suggests that a way of approximating Irenaeus's view of Adam, made from mud, is to speak of him as an earth creature.[19] Irenaeus's understanding of this earth creature is based on his combination of Genesis 1:26 with Genesis 2:7. In Genesis 1:26, we find the expression of the

---

[16] Minns, *Irenaeus: An Introduction,* 69.

[17] *AH* 3.20.2.

[18] *AH* 5.29.1.

[19] Minns, *Irenaeus: An Introduction,* 70.

divine intention in creating the human: "Let us make human-kind in our image, according to our likeness." In Genesis 2:7 we see how God carries out this intention by creating the earth creature (*adam*) from the dust of the ground (*adamah*), and breathing into this creature's nostrils the breath of life. The human, Irenaeus concludes, is made in the image and likeness of God from the mud of the earth.

The making of the human from mud in the divine image is a fully trinitarian act for Irenaeus. God creates the earth creature by means of the two Hands of the Word and Wisdom. Unlike most of the later Christian tradition, Irenaeus identifies Wisdom with the Spirit. The one and only transcendent God, then, creates the earth creatures immediately through the divine Word and Spirit, with no need for intermediaries such as angels or other powers:

> It was not angels, therefore, who made us, nor who formed us, neither had angels power to make an image of God, not anyone else, except the Word of the Lord, nor any Power remotely distant from the Father of all things. For God did not stand in need of these [beings], in order for the accomplishing of what he had himself determined with himself beforehand should be done, as if he did not possess his two hands. For with him were always present the Word and Wisdom, the Son and the Spirit, by whom and in whom, freely and spon-taneously, he made all things, to whom also he speaks, saying, "Let us make the human being after our image and likeness."[20]

Irenaeus often refers to the human creature as the *plasma* of God, a word that in both Latin and Irenaeus's original Greek means something molded or formed. The human is the *handi-work* of God, molded and formed by the two Hands of Word

---

[20] *AH* 4.20.1.

and Spirit. All creatures are in the Hands of God, and each human being is constantly held in the Hands of God and continually shaped by these Hands.

At the center of Irenaeus's thought is the relation between *Adam*, the earth creature, and the Word of God who comes in the flesh. He takes up Paul's idea that Adam is the "type" of the one to come (Rom 5:14). As I have already noted, it is characteristic of Irenaeus that the only perspective from which the beginning of creation can be understood is that of the end, the Word of the Cross, and the final transformation of all things in Christ.[21] The preexistent Word is the true beginning of creation, but this true beginning appears only at the end. Irenaeus writes:

> Hence Paul, too, styled Adam *a type of the one who is to come*, because the Word as Artisan of all things had designed beforehand, with a view to himself, the future economy relating to the Son of God on behalf of the human race; namely God destined the first, the ensouled human [Adam], that he might be saved by the spiritual human [Christ]. For inasmuch as the Savior existed beforehand, it was necessary that what was to be saved should also exist, so that the Savior would not be something without a purpose.[22]

Irenaeus expands Paul's typological correlation between Adam and Christ, so that it becomes an "all-embracing economy of God, understanding the end in terms of the beginning, with the end in turn shedding light on the beginning."[23] Through the Word, and the breath of God, mud is first brought to life in Adam. But then "the last Adam became a life-giving spirit" (1 Cor 15:45), and in Christ, the second Adam, the Spirit vivifies the human creature for communion with God.

---

[21] Behr, *Irenaeus of Lyons*, 145.

[22] *AH* 1.22.3.

[23] Behr, *Irenaeus of Lyons*, 122.

What is first expressed as the divine intention, to create the human in the image and likeness of God (Gen 1:26), and then is begun, when God molds the human from mud by the two Hands, is fulfilled in Christ, the true image and the truly living human being: "What is sketched out in Adam, clay animated by a breath of life, is brought to perfection by Christ, vivified by the Holy Spirit, the Hands of God through whom God himself has been at work throughout the whole economy."[24] Irenaeus can agree with the claim of his opponents that of themselves, "flesh and blood cannot inherit the kingdom of God" (1 Cor 15:20), but he insists against them that fleshly creatures can and do inherit the kingdom because of the two Hands of God. Importantly, for Irenaeus, we are not saved *from* flesh and blood, but rather we are created and re-created *in and through* flesh and blood, beginning with that of Christ.[25]

As Minns points out, while today we tend to think of biblical typology as something from the First Testament that prefigures something in the new dispensation of Christ, Irenaeus, by contrast, thinks of a type in a literal Greek sense, as an impression or imprint, like the impression made in wax by a seal. Adam, then, does not simply prefigure Christ, but rather Adam's bodily humanity is shaped *according* to Christ's bodily humanity. This means that, in Irenaeus's thought, "Adam was consequent on Christ, not the other way round."[26]

Irenaeus can speak in various ways about the image and likeness of God in the human, but in a particularly striking way he proposes a twofold understanding of this image and likeness. First, when God shaped the human from mud, God did so after the pattern of the body of the incarnate Word. We are in the *image* of God, then, because our *bodies* are modeled on the body of Christ.[27] And second, when through baptism

---

[24] Ibid., 123.

[25] Ibid.

[26] Minns, *Irenaeus: An Introduction*, 100.

[27] *Demonstration*, 22. AH 5.16.2.

the Spirit of God bathes our bodies with the light that radiates from the flesh of the risen Christ, we will come to the *likeness* of God, sharing in incorruptibility.[28]

Although he can say that humans are created in the image and likeness of God, it is characteristic of Irenaeus to see the human, created in the divine image, as intended to come to the full likeness of God only through a gradual process of development. He thinks of the first humans as young and inexperienced. He takes Adam and Eve's youthful disobedience seriously, and sees it, and death, as defeated and overcome in the obedience of Christ on the cross. In his view, however, the likeness to God was easily lost because of the youthful immaturity of the human and because the divine economy had not yet reached its fulfillment. Strikingly, he specifies a further specific reason for the disobedience of the human and the loss of the likeness to God—it is because the enfleshed Word who is the true image, "after whose image the human had been created," had not yet appeared in our history and become visible. Because the true Image had not yet appeared in the flesh, the human "easily lost the likeness."[29]

Incarnation and Recapitulation

Like the word *economy*, the word *recapitulation* was widely used in the Greek schools of rhetoric. In these schools the *recapitulation* was the restatement of the whole argument, the summing up, the epitome or résumé, which brings all the details of the presentation into a unified and complete picture. In the New Testament, Paul can speak of all the diverse commandments of the Law as being recapitulated in the words of Jesus: "Love your neighbor as yourself" (Rom 13:9). In Ephesians we hear that God's economy, God's plan that involves creation and redemption, is for all things to be recapitulated

---

[28] *AH* 5.6.1; 7.2; 8.1.
[29] *AH* 5.16.2.

in Christ: "With all wisdom and insight he has made known to us the mystery of his will, according to his good pleasure that he set forth in Christ, as a plan [economy] for the fullness of times, to sum up [recapitulate] all things in him, things in heaven and things on earth" (Eph 1:9–10). God has put all things under the feet of the risen Christ, and "made him the head [recapitulation] over all things for the church, which is his body, the fullness of him who fills all in all" (Eph 1:22).[30]

It is important to note the literary/rhetorical background for Irenaeus's use of the word *recapitulation*. In a particular way it is the written word, the Scripture, which is recapitulated in the gospel of Christ. All the various words of Scripture are recapitulated in the Word made flesh, whom Irenaeus sees as the "concise Word" of God, in and for the world.[31] The whole of Scripture speaks of the Word of God, but the very prolixity of the Scripture makes the Word obscure. So Irenaeus says that the gospel of Christ "cuts short" the Law and reveals salvation "according to the brevity of faith and love."[32] This gospel is the Word proclaimed authentically in the tradition and life of the church. While the Scripture speaks of the work of God in Christ at length and diachronically, the gospel synchronically recapitulates the Scriptures as the concise Word of God.[33]

Irenaeus's view of the whole biblical account speaking synchronically of Christ is captured in two of his images. The first, which I have already mentioned, is the image of the Scriptures as a beautiful mosaic of a king, made by a skillful artist from precious jewels.[34] The mosaic is distorted when tiles are broken or displaced. Irenaeus sees his opponents as distorting the mosaic when they pick and choose particular texts to support their Valentian views. It is only the gospel proclaimed in the

---

[30] See also Eph. 4:15; Col. 1:18; 2:10.

[31] *Demonstration*, 87. See Behr, *Irenaeus of Lyons*, 124–44.

[32] *Demonstration*, 87.

[33] Behr, *Irenaeus of Lyons*, 139.

[34] *AH* 1.8.1.

Christian community that enables us to see the whole of the Scriptures as the brilliant portrait of Christ. Irenaeus's second image of a proper synchronic reading of the Scriptures is the parable of the treasure hidden in a field (Mt 13:34).[35] When the Scriptures are read by Christians in the light of the gospel of Christ proclaimed in the church, Irenaeus proposes, it is Christ who is the treasure hidden in the Scriptures, and it is the cross of Christ that brings this treasure to light.

In his treatment of the incarnation in *The Demonstration of the Apostolic Preaching*, Irenaeus concludes his extensive review of the Scriptures, presented as preparation for salvation in Christ, by referring to the recapitulation text from Ephesians 1:10. At the close of the age, the Word of God is now revealed as the human one "recapitulating all things" in himself, "things in heaven and things on earth." This recapitulation occurs in the new, radical communion between the human and God that occurs in Jesus. If it were not for the Word's coming to us in the flesh, Irenaeus says, we would be "unable to have any participation in incorruptibility."[36] Although we are implicated in the flesh we take from Adam, and are bound to death through his disobedience, we are now liberated by the obedience of the Word in the flesh: "The Word became flesh, that by means of the flesh which sin has mastered and seized and dominated, by this, it might no longer be in us."[37]

In Irenaeus's thought it is essential that the Word received the same embodiment (*sárkōsis*) as the first-formed Adam, so that the Word might "vanquish in Adam what has struck us in Adam."[38] As God took mud from the ground and fashioned the first earth creature, so now "recapitulating" this first human being, the new Adam "receives the same arrangement

---

[35] *AH* 1.26.1.

[36] *Demonstration*, 31.

[37] Ibid.

[38] Ibid.

[*oikonomía*] of embodiment [*sárkōsis*]."[39] Irenaeus sees a parallel between the first human being made from virgin earth and the breath of God, and Jesus being born from the virgin Mary and of the Holy Spirit. It is because he is truly born of Mary that Christ shares the flesh of Adam: "He did not receive any other formation [*plasma*], but being born from her who was the race of Adam, he maintained the likeness of the formation."[40]

Irenaeus says that "it was necessary for Adam to be recapitulated in Christ, that 'mortality might be swallowed up in immortality.'"[41] The cross is at the center of this recapitulation, as the transgression that occurred through a tree is overcome by the tree of the cross: "So, by the means of the obedience by which he obeyed unto death, hanging upon the tree, he undid the old disobedience occasioned by the tree."[42] Then, in a remarkable text, Irenaeus proposes that the Word who was crucified in the form of a cross, is the Word who was already imprinted on all dimensions of creation. The whole creation is cruciform because of the presence and action of the creative Word of God in its length, breadth, height, and depth:

> And since he is the Word of God Almighty, who invisibly pervades the whole creation, and encompasses its length, breadth, height and depth—for by the Word of God everything is administered—so too was the Son of God crucified in these [fourfold dimensions] having been imprinted in the form of the cross in everything; for it was necessary for Him, becoming visible, to make manifest his form of the cross in everything, that he might demonstrate, by his visible form [on the cross], his activity which is on the invisible [level], for

---

[39] Ibid., 32.

[40] Ibid., 33.

[41] Ibid., referring to 2 Cor 5:4, and 1 Cor 15:54.

[42] Ibid., 34.

it is he who illumines the heights, that is, the things in heaven, and holds the "deep," which is beneath the earth, stretches the "length" from the East to the West, and who navigates the "breadth" of the northern and southern regions, inviting the dispersed from all sides to the knowledge of the Father.[43]

Minns says that the Word of the cross "mirrors the cruciform stamp of his presence in the universe—stretching throughout the whole of creation, holding every part of it in existence."[44] Behr, too, interprets Irenaeus as saying that the Word of God who adorned and arranged the heavens and the earth does so in a "cruciform manner."[45] For Irenaeus, the whole creation is understood as the handiwork of the Word, who by means of this handiwork reveals the Creator.[46] It is this same Word of creation who is engaged with Abraham, Moses, and all the economies recounted in the Scriptures. In Jesus Christ, the Word who is "always present with the human race" is now united with and grafted to the Word's own handiwork. This is the Word made flesh who "suffered for us and rose for our sakes, and who will come again in the Father's glory *to raise up all flesh*."[47] In his death and resurrection, the incarnate Word recapitulates, saves, and brings to fulfillment, all things:

There is therefore as we have shown, one God the Father and one Christ Jesus our Lord, who comes through every economy and *recapitulates in himself all things*. Now humanity, too, God's handiwork, is contained in this "all." So he also recapitulated in himself

---

[43] Ibid. Irenaeus seems to be building on Justin, in his *First Apology* 60, who took a lead from Plato, in *Timaeus* 36B.

[44] Minns, *Irenaeus: An Introduction*, 109.

[45] Behr, *Irenaeus of Lyons*, 135.

[46] *AH* 4.6.6.

[47] *AH* 3.16.6.

humanity; the invisible becoming visible; the incomprehensible, comprehensible, the impassible, passible; the Word, the human. Thus *he recapitulated in himself all things*, so that just as the Word of God is the sovereign ruler over supercelestial, spiritual and invisible beings, so he might possess sovereign rule over visible and corporeal things; and thus, by taking to himself the primacy, and constituting himself head of the church, he might draw all things to himself in the proper time.[48]

Irenaeus insists, then, that this transforming recapitulation involves not just spiritual reality, but "visible and corporeal things." He strongly resists disembodied theologies. What happens in Christ involves "all things"—the whole visible, material, biological, and human world. Irenaeus is clearly focused on the human, but as the above quotation makes clear, the human is part of the wider "all things," which are recapitulated in Christ. Thomas Torrance sums up the meaning of recapitulation as it applies to the whole creation, from its beginning to its final fulfillment:

"Recapitulation" means that redemptive activity of God in Jesus Christ was not just a transcendent act that touched our existence in space and time at one point, but an activity that passed into our existence and is at work within it, penetrating back to the beginning in the original creation retracing and reaffirming in it the divine Will, and reaching forward to the consummation in the new creation in which all things are gathered up, thus connecting the end with the beginning.[49]

---

[48] *AH* 3.16.6.

[49] Thomas F. Torrance, *Divine Meaning: Studies in Patristic Hermeneutics* (Edinburgh: T&T Clark, 1995), 121.

Creation's Transformation—
The Kingdom of the Son

Irenaeus does not think of creation as something static. For him it is oriented from the beginning toward its proper goal, which is the incarnate Word and the promised Kingdom: "Creation is not stagnant, but ever maturing and advancing towards that *telos* which since the genesis has been the intended point of fulfilment, and which is fully revealed in the incarnate Christ's promise of an eternal kingdom."[50] Irenaeus sees the six days of creation as pointing to the great eras of the economy of salvation that will culminate in the cosmic Sabbath, in which the creation will rest in its fulfillment. Then Christ will both "renew the inheritance of the earth" and, in the resurrection of the flesh, restore the glory of the children of God.[51]

Inspired by the apocalyptic texts of the Bible, Irenaeus expects the Antichrist to establish a kingdom in Jerusalem for three and a half years, and Christ to come to defeat and overthrow the Antichrist. Then the just will rise from the dead to dwell in the Kingdom of the Son. At the end of this period, the Son will hand the Kingdom over to the Father. There will be a new heaven and a new earth, and the heavenly Jerusalem will come down to the new earth.[52] Irenaeus follows Papias ("a hearer of John and a companion of Polycarp") in seeing the economy as directed toward an earthly kingdom that involved a renewal of earth, the raising of the dead, and the coming of the risen Christ to dwell on earth for a thousand years.[53] In the century after Irenaeus, more Platonic theologians like Origen would find this millennial vision too bodily and earthly, and

---

[50] M. C. Steenberg, *Irenaeus on Creation: The Cosmic Christ and the Saga of Redemption* (Leiden and Boston: Brill, 2008), 52.

[51] *AH* 5.33.1.

[52] *AH* 5.35.2.

[53] *AH* 5.33.4.

replace it with a far more spiritual theology. But Irenaeus's whole stance was based on a positive view of material creation, the human body, and the incarnation. He never supported any kind of spiritualizing interpretation of the coming kingdom.[54] With his view of the economy as centering on the body made from mud, Irenaeus explicitly rejects the idea that the promise of the resurrection can be explained away in any kind of allegorical or spiritual interpretation.[55]

In his view, it is appropriate and proper that those who have toiled and suffered in this material creation "will rise again to behold God" in this very same creation, and that this creation will itself be renewed.[56] It seems only proper to him that the saints who were slain for the love of God in this creation should be brought to life in this same creation. Quoting Romans 8 on the creation being delivered from the bondage of corruption, Irenaeus speaks of the whole creation as being restored to its primeval condition and placed under the dominion of the righteous.[57] He sees this restoration as the fulfillment of the promise of the land made long ago to Abraham. While Abraham did not receive the land in his lifetime, the promise will be fulfilled when he and all his offspring ("those who fear God and believe in him") receive the gift of the land in the renewed earth at the resurrection.[58]

Irenaeus envisions the restored land as gloriously fruitful: "the creation, having been renovated and set free, shall fructify with an abundance of all kinds of food, from the dew of heaven, and from the fertility of the earth."[59] He describes the abundance of a renewed nature with extraordinary images of fruitfulness:

---

[54] Minns, *Irenaeus: An Introduction*, 142.

[55] *AH* 5.35.1–2.

[56] *AH* 5.32.1–2.

[57] *AH* 5.32.2.

[58] Ibid.

[59] *AH* 5.33.3.

The days will come, in which vines shall grow, each having ten thousand branches, and each branch ten thousand twigs, and in each true twig then thousand shoots,
and in each one of the shoots ten thousand clusters,
and on every one of the clusters ten thousand grapes,
and every grape when pressed will give five and twenty
metretes of wine . . . [the Lord declared] that a grain of
wheat would produce ten thousand ears, and that every
ear should have ten thousand grains, and every grain
should yield ten pounds of clear, pure, fine flour; and
that all other fruit-bearing trees, and seeds and grass,
would produce in similar proportions.[60]

In this renewed land there will be peace among the animals:
"All animals feeding [only] on the production of the earth,
should [in those days] become peaceful and harmonious
among each other, and be in perfect subjection to the human."
For Irenaeus, this interpretation is well grounded in the tradition: it is "borne witness to in writing, by Papias, the hearer of
John, and a companion of Polycarp." Peace among the animals
will fulfill the promise of Isaiah 11:6–9, that the wolf will live
with the lamb, the lion will eat straw like the ox, and there will
be no harm done on all God's holy mountain. Irenaeus is well
aware that some people see this promise as referring to violent
human beings of different nations coming to peace. Nevertheless, he insists that, in the resurrection of the just, these words
will also apply to the animals, for "God is rich in all things."[61]

Irenaeus resists allegorical or spiritual interpretation of the
biblical promises. Without question, he says, these promises
apply to the resurrection of the just to dwell in the Kingdom
of the Son. The heavenly Jerusalem will descend to earth, and
there will be a new heaven and a new earth. Irenaeus insists
that the new heaven and new earth (Is 65:17; Rev 21:1) will

---

[60] Ibid.
[61] *AH* 5.33.4.

not involve the annihilation of the present earth. He gives an important place to the text from First Corinthians: "The present form of this world is passing away" (1 Cor 7:31). This means, he says, that "neither is the substance nor the essence of the creation annihilated," for the God who created it is faithful and true. It is only the "fashion" or current form of the world that will pass away.

As there will be real human beings in the resurrection of the just, so must there be a real establishment (*plantationem*), or world that they inhabit, so that they do not "vanish away among non-existent things, but progress among those that have an actual existence."[62] When the fashion of this world passes away, when the human being has been renewed and flourishes in incorruptibility, then "there shall be the new heaven and the new earth, in which the new human shall remain [continually], always holding fresh converse with God."[63]

Irenaeus sees some of the just as entering the new heaven, others the garden of paradise, and others the holy city, but all will see God and grow in their capacity to know and love God. They will ascend through the Spirit to the Son and through the Son to the Father, and the Son will hand over the Kingdom to the Father.[64] Irenaeus concludes his *Against Heresies* by recalling the biblical promises of the resurrection of the just, the inheritance of the kingdom of the earth, the Lord sharing with his disciples the new cup in the kingdom, and the creation being set free from its bondage to corruption to share the liberty of the children of God. He celebrates the wonder of the mysteries of God, unknown to angels, of the marvelous way that the human, God's handiwork, is brought to fulfillment. The Word, who "contains" all creatures, descends to the creature, to what has been molded (*plasma*). And the Word is made flesh, that "the creature should contain the Word, and

---

[62] Ibid.
[63] Ibid.
[64] *AH* 5.36.2.

ascend to him, passing beyond the angels, and be made after the image and likeness of God."[65]

God's Transcendent Greatness and God's Down-to-Earth Love

Irenaeus has a commitment to divine transcendence that is even more radical than the view of his opponents—for him there is no hierarchy of transcendence, simply the world of creatures and the one fully transcendent God. Whereas his gnostic opponents see the divine and creaturely as on a continuum, the great chain of being, for Irenaeus there is absolutely no continuity between God and creation: "Rather, God is the only reality, the only thing that really *is*, and over against God, called into existence out of nothingness by God, and held in being, poised over nothingness by God, is everything that God creates."[66] The good God creates all things ex nihilo. God simply is, while the whole world of creatures comes into being through God's action and exists only from God.[67]

Because of the divine transcendence, God can be intimately present to creatures, immediately bestowing existence on them. As Irenaeus says, all creatures are in the hands of God.[68] He often expresses the radical transcendence of God through an axiom from *The Shepherd of Hermas,* which states that God contains all things and is contained by none. Irenaeus writes, for example: "Truly, then, the Scripture declared, which says, 'First of all, believe that there is one God, who has established all things, and completed them, and having caused that from what had no being, all things should come into existence': He who *contains all things and is himself contained by no one*."[69]

---

[65] *AH* 5.34.3.

[66] Minns, *Irenaeus: An Introduction,* 42.

[67] Ibid., 43.

[68] *AH* 4.19.2; 20.1.

[69] *AH* 4.20.2, emphasis added. The Scripture to which Irenaeus refers here is from the *Shepherd of Hermas.*

Irenaeus consistently repeats that God is without limits, is contained by nothing, yet contains all that exists. This uncontained and incomprehensible God is the true infinite fullness beyond all things. How can there be contact between such a God and creatures? How can we human creatures possibly know a God of such radical transcendence?

Michael Slusser has pointed to the way Irenaeus resolves this issue: the apparently insuperable metaphysical obstacle constituted by divine transcendence is overcome purely by the loving initiative of God.[70] What resolves the metaphysical obstacle is divine love, usually rendered as *dilectio* in the old Latin translation of Irenaeus's *Against Heresies*. Irenaeus responds to the apparent distance between the transcendent God and the world of creatures by systematically bringing together God's greatness (*magnitudo*) and God's love (*dilectio*). Slusser proposes that this systematic understanding of the relationship between God and creation is Irenaeus's most creative contribution to Christian theology.[71]

Irenaeus certainly sees God the Creator, the Father of all, unlike the chaotic Aeons of the Gnostic hierarchy, as far beyond human passions and conflicts. He points out that when we use words such as *intelligence* and *light* of God, we do so only in a way that points to what is far beyond our limited human meanings of these words. He then explains the condition under which we can rightly use these words of God: "He is spoken of in these terms according to love [*secundum dilectionem*]; according to greatness [*secundum magnitudinem*]; however, he is understood to be above them."[72] The God beyond human language makes God's self known in love, in Jesus Christ the Word made flesh. Irenaeus's opponents

---

[70] Michael Slusser, "The Heart of Irenaeus's Theology," in *Irenaeus: Life, Scripture, Legacy*, ed. Sara Parvis and Paul Foster (Minneapolis: Fortress, 2012), 133–39.

[71] Ibid., 133.

[72] *AH* 2.13.4.

attempt to defend the transcendence of God by isolating the divine completely from the created world. Such a God does not create, save, or communicate with creatures. Irenaeus, by contrast, insists that the Creator is the true and only God, "who is unknowable in terms of greatness, but who so loves creatures as to find a way to be known by them."[73] The way that God finds is, of course, the incarnation.

Following Slusser, I will draw further attention to the way Irenaeus maintains the *magnitudo/dilectio* pairing in three quotations from the extraordinary chapter 20 of book 4 of *Against the Heresies*. At the beginning of this chapter Irenaeus combines the *magnitudo/dilectio* pairing with the axiom that God is uncontained and contains all things:

> Therefore according to greatness [*secundum magnitudinem*] there is no knowing God, for it is impossible for the Father to be measured. But according to his love [*secundum dilectionen*]—for this is what leads us through his word to God—those who obey him are always learning that God is so great [*tantus*], and that it is he who through himself established and chose and adorned and contains all things—including in this "all things" us and this world of ours. And we therefore were created along with those things contained by him.[74]

If one thinks only of the divine greatness, then knowledge of God would be impossible. But the love of God that finds expression in the Word made flesh provides a completely different result. And part of this knowledge that we have in Christ concerns this Word's creation of all things, including ourselves along with the rest of the natural world. This creative act

---

[73] Slusser, "The Heart of Irenaeus's Theology," 137.

[74] *AH* 4.20.1. For each of these texts I am following Slusser's translation in his "The Heart of Christian Theology."

of God, we are told in our next text, occurs through God's Word and Wisdom (the Spirit):

> Therefore there is one God, who made and finished all things by Word and Wisdom. But this is the Creator [*Demiurgus*], who also entrusted this world to the human race, who according to greatness [*secundum magnitudinem*] indeed is unknown to all of his creatures (for no one has searched out his height, neither of the ancients nor of those who are alive today); but according to love [*secundum dilectionem*] he is always known through him through whom he established all things. This is the Word, our Lord Jesus Christ, who in the last times became a human being among human beings, in order to join the end to the beginning, that is, humanity to God.[75]

In the Word made flesh, the communion between God and humanity takes place, God converses with human beings, God is present to creation, and God can be perceived by creatures. It becomes clear that Irenaeus is not simply talking about a knowing of God from an observation of the natural world, which might lead to the conclusion that God is, without leading to a knowing of God's true character.[76] The knowledge Irenaeus speaks of is a loving knowledge given in the Word of God, the Word through whom all things are created, who is the Word made flesh. For Irenaeus it is important to note that this is the same Word that appears in the ancient biblical promises and which enabled the prophets to speak of the divine economy of the Word made visible in Christ:

> The prophets foretold that God would be seen by human beings—as the Lord said, "Blessed are the clean

---

[75] *AH* 4.20.4.

[76] Slusser, "The Heart of Irenaeus's Theology," 137–38.

of heart, for they shall see God" [Mt 5:8]. But according to his greatness [*magnitudinem*], and inexpressible glory, "no one will see God and live." For the Father cannot be contained. But according to love [*dilectionem*] and humanity, and because he can do all things, to those who love him he grants even this, namely to see God, which is what the prophets prophesied, because "things impossible to human beings are possible to God." Human beings cannot see God on their own. But he voluntarily will be visible to human beings to whom he wills and when he will and how he wills.[77]

The love of which Irenaeus speaks is not simply God's love for us, but also our love for God. This is the true knowledge, the true gnosis, which bridges the metaphysical abyss between Creator and all creatures. Whereas in Exodus it was said, no one can see God and live (Ex 33:22–23), Irenaeus proclaims that in Christ we do see God, and in seeing God in Christ we will truly live. Those who see God in Christ are "in God" and "receive life."[78] As Irenaeus says in the well-known text to which I have already referred: "The glory of God is the living human being, and the life of the human is in seeing God."[79] He goes on to explain that "if the manifestation of God which is made by means of the creation affords life to all living on the earth, much more does that revelation of the Father which comes through the Word, give life to those who see God."[80]

Irenaeus has no quarrel with the gnostic view of the transcendence of God. But he insists that this transcendence applies to the one God who is Creator and who creates through Word and Spirit. He also insists that his church people know the transcendent God because they know the love of God in

---

[77] *AH* 4.20.5.
[78] Ibid.
[79] *AH* 4.20.7.
[80] Ibid.

Christ. As Slusser says: "Knowledge of the creator God is possible to ordinary creatures, not because the creator is a puny, less than spiritual being, but because the immeasurable great creator God loves everything in creation and therefore gives that knowledge even to us human beings through the Word made flesh and Spirit of wisdom, according to the measure of divine love."[81]

Irenaeus and Deep Incarnation: Critical Differences, Resonances, and Insights

There are obvious differences between the theology of Irenaeus and the proponents of deep incarnation, and also strong resonances, where insights from Irenaeus can offer a theological foundation for the development of deep incarnation.

Critical Differences

- Irenaeus's theology was dealing with issues confronting him in his own time, theologies like those of Marcion and Valentinus, and not issues raised by the twenty-first-century ecological crisis and contemporary evolutionary science. Obviously, then, we cannot expect his theology to directly respond to contemporary issues.
- Irenaeus's assumptions about the historicity of Genesis and the literal understandings of apocalyptic millennial expectations are not a good fit with contemporary theology.
- Irenaeus was not focused on the issue of suffering that is built into the natural world, although he was focused on death and its transformation in the cross and resurrection of the incarnate Word. Although he has a strong theology of divine love for creatures, and of Christ's love for creatures expressed on the cross, and although

---

[81] Slusser, "The Heart of Irenaeus's Theology," 139.

he believes that the cross has meaning for the whole creation, Irenaeus does not write of God suffering with suffering creatures.

Resonances and Foundational Insights

- Irenaeus has a radically incarnational theology, in which the divine act of creation is always directed toward incarnation. Creation, incarnation, and final fulfillment are united in the intention and the one economy of God. For Irenaeus the incarnation is not a "plan B"; his vision begins from the incarnate Christ of the cross and encompasses the whole creation.

- His theology of *all things* being recapitulated in Christ clearly involves not only humanity but the whole creation, and can offer a strong Patristic foundation for contemporary theologies of deep incarnation.

- Although he has a strong focus on the human, in both creation and salvation, he consistently sees the human in the context of the wider creation, and thinks that humans can exist only in the context of a real implantation in the world that they inhabit.

- He has an eschatology that unambiguously involves animals and plants and the land itself. The resurrection of Christ involves the fulfillment and transformation of "all things"—the whole visible, material, biological, and human world. When interpreted critically, his theology offers support for a contemporary theology of deep resurrection. Hans Urs von Balthasar says of Irenaeus: "In his eschatology Irenaeus produces an important counterweight to the flight from the world and the failure to take seriously the resurrection of the flesh which marks the Platonizing Christian eschatologies of a later period and indeed the average Christian consciousness."[82]

---

[82] Hans Urs von Balthasar, *The Glory of the Lord: A Theological*

- Irenaeus not only has a high view of the transcendence of the uncontained and incomprehensible God, but he also systematically brings together divine transcendence (*magnitudo*) and divine love (*dilectio*). This could be seen as a step toward a contemporary theology of a God who is fully transcendent (*magnitudo*) suffering with creatures in their suffering out of the depths of divine compassionate love (*dilectio*).
- Irenaeus insists on the goodness of creation, of matter and flesh. He strongly resists all disembodied theologies of his day and defends the earthiness and the bodily reality of incarnation, the cross, and participation in resurrection life.
- His theology of the Creator as immediately present to each creature through the two Hands, shaping and leading each of them and all together, is in clear alignment with deep incarnation.
- Irenaeus sees the cross as imprinted by the whole of reality, and in the depths of reality. He speaks of the cross of Jesus as making visible the cruciform activity of the Word of God, who acts invisibly in the height and in the depth, in the length and in the breadth of all creaturely reality. This idea can be developed in the direction of a theology of the cross as icon or sacrament of God's redemptive presence to all suffering creatures.

As promised, in the next chapter I bring Gregersen's theology into dialogue with the thought of Athanasius, concluding with a discussion of critical differences, resonances, and foundational insights as above.

Aesthetics, II. Studies in Theological Style: Clerical Styles (Edinburgh: T&T Clark, 1984), 93.

3

Athanasius on the Depths of the Incarnation

If it is the second-century Irenaeus who sets the scene for subsequent incarnational theology, it is the fourth-century Athanasius (c. 296–373) who gives this theology what many think of as its classical expression. Like Irenaeus, then, Athanasius can be a key dialogue partner for contemporary attempts at deep incarnation. Born in Alexandria, he served as a deacon, priest, and then bishop of this great city. A leading priest of Alexandria, Arius, opened up a heated controversy by bringing into question the eternity of the Word of God. In 325, as a young deacon, Athanasius accompanied his bishop, Alexander, to the Council of Nicaea, where the views of Arius were rejected and the full and eternal divinity of the Word affirmed. In 328 Athanasius became bishop of Alexandria, at about the age of thirty, and for the rest of his life was a strong advocate for the full divinity of the Word who was made flesh.

Athanasius's *On the Incarnation*

On the Incarnation is the first text in Christian history specifically devoted to the incarnation. It forms the second part of Athanasius's early double work, *Against the Greeks—On the Incarnation*. In the introduction to *Against the Greeks*,

Athanasius says of those pagans who scorn the cross of Christ: "In slandering the cross they do not see that its power has filled the whole world, and that through it the effects of the knowledge of God have been revealed to all." Speaking of those who reject and mock the worship of one who was crucified, Athanasius says that "if they really applied their minds to his divinity they would not have mocked at so great a thing, but would have recognized that he was the Savior of the universe and the cross was not the ruin but the salvation of creation."[1] Two things are important about these words in relation to the theology of deep incarnation. First, as recent commentators have noted, Athanasius's double work is first and foremost "an apology for the cross."[2] Second, from the beginning Athanasius specifies that the cross is salvific not just for human beings, but for the whole universe: Christ is "the Savior of the universe," and the cross is for "the salvation of creation."

The interrelationship between creation and salvation is central to Athanasius's theology. The Word of creation is the Word of our redemption. In the incarnation, this fully divine Word takes our bodily reality as his own and, through his death and resurrection, transforms and deifies creaturely reality. Khaled Anatolios describes the relationship between God and creation as the "architectonic center" of Athanasius's Christological vision.[3] It is Christology that radically unites God and the world of creatures.[4]

---

[1] Athanasius, *Against the Greeks*, 1, ed. and trans. Robert Thomson in *Athanasius: Contra Gentes and De Incarnatione* (Oxford: Clarendon Press, 1971), 3–5. I will cite Thomson's translation in what follows, but will adjust it slightly, replacing the generic "man" with "human" or "human being."

[2] Khaled Anatolios, *Athanasius: The Coherence of His Thought* (London: Routledge, 1998), 28; John Behr, *The Nicene Faith: Part 1: True God of True God*, The Formation of Christian Theology, vol. 2 (Crestwood, NY: St. Vladimir's Seminary Press, 2004), 171.

[3] Khaled Anatolios, *Athanasius* (London: Routledge, 2004), 39.

[4] Ibid., 40.

Athanasius looks back from the cross to the origin of evil. He sees human beings as created for communion with God. Evil is not God's will, and it did not exist from the beginning, but comes about through human sin. Humans were created to contemplate God in the Word who is revealed in creation, but they turned instead to idolatry, making creatures into gods. Athanasius goes to great lengths to describe the perversity of this history of idolatry. In opposition to all such idolatrous views, he puts forward the Christian view of the one God who creates all things through God's own Word and Wisdom. Athanasius speaks of the eternal one who is made flesh using many biblically based titles, including not only Word of God and Wisdom of God, but also Image of God, Radiance of God, and Hand of God (following Irenaeus) as well as Son of God.

This Wisdom/Word, he insists, is not a creature, but the "the very Word of the good God of the universe, who is other than created things and all creation."[5] Athanasius sees every aspect of creation as bearing the imprint of the uncreated Wisdom of God. Nothing would exist if it were not continually created by divine Wisdom:

> He, the power of God and wisdom of God, turns the heaven, has suspended the earth, and by his own will has set it resting on nothing. Illuminated by him, the sun gives light to the world, and the moon receives its measure of light. Through him water is suspended in the clouds, rains water the earth, the sea is confined, and the earth is covered with verdure in all kinds of plants.[6]

With Irenaeus, Athanasius defends creation ex nihilo. The universe of creatures is not only originally created out of nothing, but also always rests on nothing. It is held in being over an abyss of nothing through the eternal Word: "For the nature of

---

[5] Athanasius, *Against the Greeks*, 40.
[6] Ibid.

created things, having come into being from nothing, is unstable, and is weak and mortal when considered by itself."[7] But the God of all is good and kind by nature. So this good and kind God provides for the continual existence of the world of creatures through the Word. They exist by participation in the Word of God:

> After making everything by his own eternal Word and bringing creation into existence, he did not abandon it to be carried away and suffer through its own nature, lest it run the risk of returning to nothing. But being good, he governs and establishes the whole world through his Word who is himself God, in order that creation, illuminated by the leadership, providence and ordering of the Word, may be able to remain firm, since it *participates* in the Word who is truly from the Father and is aided by him to exist, and lest it suffer what would happen, I mean a relapse into nonexistence, if it were not protected by the Word.[8]

From the creaturely side, creation is an ongoing relation of participation, by which creatures exist securely because they partake of the Word of God. In the above text, Athanasius speaks of the Word of God as "bringing into existence," "governing," "establishing," "leading," "providing for," and "ordering" creation. He goes on to say that the Word is "present in all things" and "gives life and protection to everything, everywhere, to each individually and to all together."[9] It is the presence of the Word that enables creaturely existence. And it is this presence that brings all the diverse creatures of the natural

---

[7] Ibid., 41.

[8] Ibid. In this text I have modified Thompson's translation, replacing *shares* with the italicized word *participates*, as translation of Athanasius's *metalambánousa*.

[9] Ibid.

world and all the elements of nature into balance and harmony. Taking up a musical image, Athanasius says: "The Wisdom of God, holding the universe like a lyre," draws together the variety of created things, "thus producing in beauty and harmony a single world and a single order within it."[10]

In *On the Incarnation*, Athanasius tells his readers that he needs to begin his discussion of the redemption by first speaking of the creation of the universe. In this way, he says, it will become apparent that it is fitting that the renewal of creation "is effected by the Word who created it from the beginning."[11] Again he insists on creation ex nihilo. Against various competing philosophies of creation, he argues that God does not depend on preexisting matter, but rather creates the matter from which all created things come into being. Here and elsewhere, Athanasius defends his view that the Creator, who is "the Father of Christ," creates all things through the eternal Word, by pointing to the "all-inclusive" text: "All things came into being through him, and without him not one thing came into being" (Jn 1:3).[12] In his later writings, Athanasius will also vigorously defend the divinity of the Holy Spirit, and points out how the Spirit is involved with the Word in both creation and saving incarnation: "The Father creates and renews all things through the Son and in the Holy Spirit."[13]

There are two reasons for the incarnation according to Athanasius. First, in sections 3–10 of *On the Incarnation*, he discusses the incarnation as overcoming death and bringing resurrection life. Then, in sections 11–19, he describes the incarnation as renewing the image of God in human beings and so enabling them to know God. The first analysis takes the reader again to God's act of creation, where God "made

---

[10] Ibid., 42.

[11] Athanasius, *On the Incarnation*, 1.

[12] Ibid., 2.

[13] Athanasius, *Letters to Serapion*, 1:24, in Anatolios, *Athanasius*, 223–24.

everything out of nothing through his own Word, our Lord Jesus Christ." Athanasius then narrows his focus to the creation of human beings:

> And among these creatures, of all those on earth he had special pity for the human race, and seeing that by the definition of its own existence it would be unable to exist for ever, he gave it an added grace, not simply creating humans like all irrational animals on the earth, but making them in his own image and giving them also a share in the power of his own Word, so that having as it were shadows of the Word and being rational, they might be able to remain in felicity and live the true life in paradise, which is really that of the saints.[14]

Like all other creatures, humans would have been destined for death, but God gave them a special grace, making them in the divine image, empowering them by the Word, and freeing them from death. They were granted "the grace of the Word" to live a divine life, but were required to be faithful to God's command.[15] They turned away from God, rejecting God's law, and thus were reduced to their natural, mortal state, facing death and corruption. Athanasius describes how sin then increased everywhere—"they became insatiable in sinning"; "the whole earth was filled with murders and violence"; "cities warred with cities, and peoples rose up against peoples."[16]

In this context, Athanasius reflects on the divine response to sin. On the one hand, God would not be truthful if, having said that sin results in death, this failed to occur. On the other hand, it would not be worthy of the goodness of God if the human being, who had been created by God and partaken of the Word, was to be abandoned to corruption and come to

---

[14] Athanasius, *On the Incarnation*, 3.

[15] Ibid., 5.

[16] Ibid.

nothing. Athanasius asks: "What should God, who is good, have done?" God's response to this dilemma is that the Word who had created the universe from nothing would be the one to bring about new creation.[17] The Word who fills the universe embraces our creaturely reality. The creative Word takes a body like ours from the Virgin, as an instrument for our salvation, and gives his life as a sacrifice. Because of him we are destined for radically new life, sharing in the resurrection of the Word made flesh. This, Athanasius tells us, "is the primary cause of the incarnation of the Savior."[18]

The second reason for the incarnation is that humans might know God. Without the incarnation of the Word, humans would have had no real knowledge or understanding of the God who created them, or of the Word by whom they had been made. Originally God had made them in the divine image and likeness so that "they might be able through him (the Word of God) to gain some notion about the Father, and recognizing the Maker, might live a happy and truly blessed life."[19] But, in turning from God, they lost the proper knowledge of God, and made idols for themselves.

Even so, Athanasius notes, God had not hidden God's self, but had provided manifold ways of self-revelation to humans in creation itself: "They could lift their eyes to the immensity of heaven, and discerning the harmony of creation know its ruler, the Word of the Father." Furthermore, through God's gift of the law and the prophets of Israel, they could learn of "God the Creator of the universe, the Father of Christ."[20] But, despite all of this, human beings rejected the knowledge of God and chose the path of irrationality. Again, Athanasius asks: What was God to do? In the divine mercy, God would renew humanity made in the divine image in order that human

---

[17] Ibid., 7.
[18] Ibid., 10.
[19] Ibid., 11.
[20] Ibid., 12.

beings might once again be able to know God. This would occur through the coming in the body of the very Image of God, our Savior Jesus Christ. The Word is revealed in the body so that "those who were unwilling to know him by his providence and government of the universe, yet by the works done through the body might know the Word of God who was in the body, and through him the Father."[21] Humans had been led astray by their senses to worship what they could see and touch, so the Word comes in the senses, teaching the truth of God through the actions of the body, in the incarnate Word's deeds and teachings, and ultimately through his cross and resurrection. Through our senses, and in the body, we meet the Word and Wisdom of God, in all that makes up Christ's life, including the signs he does in his ministry, and his death and resurrection.

Athanasius insists that the eternal Word is not enclosed in the body of Jesus, but continues to act creatively and providentially in the whole universe. Although the Word is present to the whole universe, the Word is not contained by creation, but contains everything else: "For he was not bound to the body, but rather he controlled it, so he was in it and in everything, and outside creation, and was only at rest in the Father. And the most amazing thing is this, that he both lived as a human being and, as the Word, gave life to everything, and as the Son was with the Father."[22]

Returning to the cross of Jesus, Athanasius sees the whole creation as confessing that the one who suffered there was "Son of God and Savior of all." Creation itself is not silent at the cross but cries out:

> What is most amazing, even at his death—or rather at the victory over death, I mean the cross—the whole of creation was confessing that he who was known and

---

[21] Ibid., 14.
[22] Ibid., 17.

suffered in the body was not simply a human being, but the Son of God and Savior of all. For the sun turned back, and the earth shook, and the mountains were rent, and all were terrified; and these things showed that Christ who was on the cross was God, and that the whole of creation was his handmaid and was witnessing in fear to the coming of his master. So in this way God the Word revealed himself to human beings through his works.[23]

In this text, John Behr notes: "Creation not only witnesses to the divinity of Jesus Christ, as the one who governs and orders the creation, but, Athanasius points out, it witnesses to the divinity of the one who died on the cross."[24] This death on the cross, Athanasius goes on to say, is "the chief point of our faith" and "absolutely everyone talks about it."[25] Of course, for Athanasius, the cross involves the resurrection of the crucified Jesus. It is the transformation of our creaturely death that is its point. When Athanasius deals with the resurrection in *On the Incarnation*, his focus is not on the appearances of the risen Christ, but on the way that the body of Christ, the Church, witnesses to the resurrection: "If anyone were to watch men and women and young children eagerly rushing to death for their devotion to Christ. . . . Let no one doubt that death has been destroyed by Christ and its corruption broken and brought to an end."[26]

The witness of those who belong to the body of Christ is the prime visible "proof," for Athanasius, of the transformation of death by the cross of Christ. The works of the risen Christ are revealed in his body, in the lives of Christians. Those who live in Christ demonstrate Christ's victory over death.

---

[23] Ibid., 19.

[24] Behr, *The Nicene Faith*, part 1, vol. 1, 200.

[25] Athanasius, *On the Incarnation*, 19.

[26] Ibid., 27–30.

Behr notes that here and elsewhere, there is "an identity of the body assumed by the Word with all human beings, an identity now manifest in those who put on Christ, so giving a far broader scope, than is often done, to what is meant by incarnation."[27] The Word of creation, the one who called the creaturely world into being in the first place, is the one who renews it by coming into creation in the body, and the bodily presence of the Word is continued today in his body that is the church.

Wisdom's Ways of Being with Creatures

In a particularly rich passage in his *Orations against the Arians*, Athanasius reflects on the Wisdom of God as the Creator of all things, and on the whole creation as bearing the created imprint of Wisdom, and then goes on to show how this very same divine Wisdom becomes present to creation in an unforeseeable new way in bodily incarnation. In Jesus, in his life, death, and resurrection, the Wisdom of God becomes present to creation in a radically interior way, bringing forgiveness, overcoming death, and transforming creaturely existence from within.

Athanasius spells out this line of thought at the end of his *Second Oration against the Arians*. The context is his defense of the divinity of Wisdom—in response to opponents who insist that Wisdom is a creature on the basis of the text: "The Lord created me at the beginning of his work, the first of his acts of long ago" (Prov 8:22). Athanasius answers this biblical argument by distinguishing between the *created* imprint and reflection of Wisdom found in each creature and divine Wisdom herself:

Therefore, the only-begotten and true Wisdom of God is the creator and maker of all things. For it says: "In

---

[27] Behr, *The Nicene Faith*, part 1, vol. 2, 206.

wisdom you have made all things" and "the earth is filled with your creation" (Ps 104:24). But in order that creatures may not only be but also thrive in well-being, it pleased God to have his own Wisdom condescend to creatures. Therefore he placed in each and every creature and in the totality of creation a certain imprint [*typon*] and reflection of the Image of Wisdom, so that the things that come into being may prove to be works that are wise and worthy of God. Just as our word is an image of the Word who is Son of God, so the wisdom that comes into being within us is an image of his Wisdom, in which we attain to knowledge and understanding. Thus we become recipients of the Creator-Wisdom, and through her we are able to know her Father.[28]

Several key things are said in this text. First, God has God's own Wisdom "condescend," or come down to be with each creature in immediate presence, in the act of continuous creation, as the very source of its existence. Second, God places "in every creature and in the totality of creation" an imprint (*typon*) and reflection of Wisdom. This means that whales, koalas, and humans are all in their own distinct and interrelated ways reflections of divine Wisdom. This tree I see before me not only exists from Creator-Wisdom but also in itself is a created reflection of Wisdom, bearing Wisdom's imprint. And we might say today that the universe we know, the dynamic, expanding observable universe with its two trillion galaxies, reflects divine Wisdom and bears Wisdom's mark. And earth, our fruitful, vulnerable home, with its evolutionary history,

---

[28] Athanasius, *Orations against the Arians*, 2.78, in Anatolios, *Athanasius* (New York: Routledge, 2004), 171. Anatolios comments on his translation of personal pronouns in this text: "In Athanasius's Greek, the personal pronoun switches from feminine when the subject is Wisdom (*Sophia*) to masculine when the subject is the Word (*Logos*) or the human being (*anthropos*) which the Word became" (267n173).

with its wonderfully diverse life-forms and the seas, land, and atmosphere on which life depends, reflects the beauty of divine Wisdom and is marked by Wisdom.

Third, humans have a unique participation in Wisdom: our human experience of wisdom is an image of, and a participation in, divine Wisdom. In our experience of nature, in our interpersonal relationships, in our pursuit of justice, in our search for truth and understanding, in our pondering of the Word, in moments of silence, we can find the image of Wisdom within ourselves. We are led to Creator-Wisdom herself, and in knowing her we can know the Father. It might be said today that the growing sense in the human community that we are responsible for the well-being of the global community of life on earth is not only something stirred up by the life-giving Spirit but also a participation in Holy Wisdom. Athanasius notes, with Paul, the sad fact that despite God's attributes being evident in the creation since the beginning, human beings have over and over failed to glorify God and have instead worshipped false gods (Rom 1:19–21). However, God does not abandon humanity, but out of the abundance of divine generosity sends Wisdom to be with us in the flesh:

> For God willed to make himself known no longer as in previous times through the image and shadow of wisdom, which is in creatures, but has made the true Wisdom herself take flesh and become a mortal human being and endure the death of the cross, so that henceforth all those who put their faith in him may be saved. But it is the same Wisdom of God, who previously manifested herself, and her Father through herself, by means of her image in creatures—and thus is said to be "created"—but which later on, being Word, became flesh (John 1:14) as John said.[29]

---

[29] Athanasius, *Orations against the Arians* 2.78, in Anatolios, *Athanasius*, 174.

When Athanasius says that since the incarnation God no longer reveals God's self though the image of Wisdom in creation, I take him to mean that God is no longer revealed only in this limited way but is now revealed in the utter extravagance of Wisdom made flesh. In the light of the incarnation, we have all the more reason to recognize and to celebrate Wisdom's presence in the icons of Wisdom all around us, in great trees, tiny wildflowers, threatened species, and human beings.

Deification

Athanasius makes use of a range of biblical images to interpret the meaning of the death and resurrection of Christ, which he finds in Paul and in Hebrews. At a fundamental level he sees salvation in terms of a new kind of relationship, a profound new unity between God and humanity and the wider creation. Through the incarnation, God is joined to creaturely reality in a radically immediate and internal way, for the sake of bringing creatures into the intimacy of the divine trinitarian life.

It is typical of Athanasius to insist that the Word and the Spirit are not creatures but fully divine, by saying that whereas creation is *external* to God, the Word and Spirit are *proper* to God. With the incarnation he radically reverses this language. In the incarnation, the created human body of Christ is now *proper* to, and not *external* to, the Word. This means that in the incarnation there is a radical refiguring of the externality of creation. In the incarnation it is now proper for Christ to be joined both to the Father, in the one divine nature, and to our creaturely humanity, in the flesh taken by the Word. "It is by being joined to both Christ and humanity that Christ can effectively join us to God."[30] Anatolios points to the importance of the model of predication in Athanasius's theology of salvation. In the incarnation the human condition is predicated as proper to the Word. It belongs to the subjectivity of the

---

[30] Anatolios, *Athanasius: The Coherence of His Thought*, 139.

Word. Creaturely humanity is thus now ascribed to the Word. It is "made Word" or "Worded."[31]

Athanasius has a paradoxical view of the suffering of the Word made flesh. On the one hand he holds that the Word is fully divine and is therefore impassible. On the other hand he holds that the sufferings of Jesus are to be attributed not simply to the bodily humanity but to the subjectivity of the Word. Thus Athanasius can say that the Word both suffers and does not suffer.[32] It is fundamental to see that this paradox is at the heart of his theology of salvation. The Word enters into suffering in order to transform it. Transformation is intrinsic to Athanasius's view of incarnation. As John Behr says, for Athanasius incarnation is a reciprocal and transforming dynamic.[33] He speaks of the Word as Maker and Creator, coming in a creature, in order that "he may present the world to the Father, and give peace to all, in heaven and on earth."[34] The coming of the Word to creation, then, is not a one-way event located in the past, but intrinsically a transformation of the creation, which is already evident in the church, the body of Christ.[35]

Athanasius often speaks of this transforming effect of incarnation in the language of deification. This appears first in the well-known passage of his *On the Incarnation*: "For he became human that we might become divine."[36] Athanasius uses deification language, the verb *theopoiéō*, and the noun he coins, *theopoiēsis*, far more often in his later anti-Arian writing, to defend the real divinity of the Word, who is made flesh that we might be made divine: "So he was not a human

---

[31] Ibid., 142.

[32] Ibid., 144–45.

[33] John Behr, "Saint Athanasius on 'Incarnation,'" in *Incarnation: On the Scope and Depth of Christology*, ed. Niels Henrik Gregersen (Minneapolis: Fortress, 2015), 79–98, at 97.

[34] Athanasius, *Letter to Adelphius* 8, in Anatolios, *Athanasius*, 242.

[35] Behr, "Saint Athanasius on 'Incarnation,'" 97.

[36] Athanasius, *On the Incarnation*, 54.

being and later became God. But, being God, he later became a human being in order that we may be divinized."[37]

In developing his theology of deification, Athanasius builds on Irenaeus and others, but he uses deification language more often than his predecessors, clarifies its meaning, and often pairs it with synonyms, such as adoption, renewal, salvation, sanctification, grace, transcendence, illumination, and vivification.[38] Since the Word is eternally divine and the source of deification, Athanasius insists against his opponents that the Word of God is not deified. Importantly, however, he holds that the bodily humanity of Jesus *is* deified by its union with the Word, and it is this that enables the deification of humanity.[39]

Salvation Involves the Wider Natural World

This process of salvation and deification embraces more than humanity. Athanasius sees the incarnation as bringing about a transformation in creaturely reality, a transformation already at work not only in human beings but also in the wider creation. Although his focus is on humanity, he seems naturally to include the wider creation. In the following example he refers explicitly to Romans 8:19–23 and Colossians 1:15–20, and clearly includes the whole creation in the liberation that comes through Christ's resurrection:

> The truth that refutes them is that he is called "firstborn among many brothers" (Rom 8:29) because of the kinship of the flesh, and "firstborn from the dead" (Col 1:18) because the resurrection of the dead comes

---

[37] Athanasius, *Orations against the Arians*, 1.39, in Anatolios, *Athanasius*, 96.

[38] See N. Russell, *The Doctrine of Deification in the Greek Patristic Tradition* (Oxford: Oxford University Press, 2004), 177–78.

[39] Athanasius, *Orations against the Arians*, 1.42, in Anatolios, *Athanasius*, 99.

from him and after him, and "firstborn of all creation" (Col 1:15) because of the Father's love for humanity, on account of which he not only gave consistence to all things in his Word but brought it about that the creation itself, of which the apostle says that it "awaits the revelation of the children of God," will at a certain point be delivered "from the bondage of corruption into the glorious freedom of the children of God" (Rom 8:19, 21).[40]

In another example, this time defending the full divinity of the Spirit, he insists that both Word and Spirit are at work in the bodily incarnation of the Word, for the sake of uniting and reconciling the whole creation with the Father:

Thus also when the Word visited the holy Virgin Mary, the Spirit came to her with him, and the Word in the Spirit formed the body and accommodated it to himself, out of a desire to join and present the created order to the Father through himself, and *to reconcile all things in himself, making peace between the things that are in heaven and the things that are on earth* (Col 1:20).[41]

Athanasius speaks more generally of creation being deified, often in the context of the divine adoption of human beings: "In him [the Spirit] the Word divinizes all that has come into existence. And the one in whom creatures are divinized cannot himself be external to the divinity of the Father."[42] Even if Athanasius's focus is on the human, he is not interested in making sharp distinctions between humanity and the rest of

---

[40] Ibid., 2.63.

[41] Athanasius, *Letters to Serapion*, 1.31, in Anatolios, *Athanasius*, 231–32.

[42] Athanasius, *Letters to Serapion*, 1.25, in Anatolios, *Athanasius*, 225.

creation. From the texts mentioned earlier, which refer directly to the wider natural world, it is clear that Athanasius's view is inclusive. The Word is made flesh that human beings might be forgiven, deified, and adopted as beloved sons and daughters and that the rest of creation might be transformed in Christ in its own proper way. Late in his life Athanasius writes of Christ as "the Liberator of all flesh and of all creation (cf. Rom. 8.21)," and as "the Creator and Maker coming to be in a creature so that, by granting freedom to all in himself, he may present the world to the Father and give peace to all, in heaven and on earth."[43]

The Self-Humbling God Who Transcends Transcendence

Athanasius has a radical view of the immediacy of God the Trinity to all creatures, which is closely related to his insistence on the full divinity of the Word and the Spirit. He directly opposes a dominant assumption of his time, shaped by Platonic philosophy and shared by many Christians, including opponents such as Arius, Eusebius of Caesarea, and Asterius. In this widely held assumption a created intermediary, such as the Logos, is needed between the all-holy transcendent God and created entities. Creatures then participate in the Logos, and the Logos participates in God, but is less than the all-holy and eternal God.

For many of Athanasius's contemporaries, the very transcendent otherness of God seemed to make the idea of a direct and immediate relationship between God and creatures unthinkable. On the one hand, such an immediate connection would seem to compromise the divine transcendence of the all-holy God who is radically beyond all creatures. On the other hand, from the perspective of the creature, it seemed impossible that creatures could bear the unmediated touch of

---

[43] Athanasius, *To Adelphius*, 4, in Anatolios, *Athanasius*, 238.

the all-holy God. It was necessary to them that there be some kind of "buffer" between God and the world of creatures.[44]

For Athanasius there is no buffer. In his view there is no intermediary between God and God's creatures. God is immediately present through the Word and in the Spirit, and Word and Spirit are fully divine, sharing fully in the unchanging divine nature. Athanasius shares with his opponents a conviction of the radical otherness of the Creator. How, then, is this ontological gulf between God and creatures bridged? As for Irenaeus, the gulf is bridged by God alone. There is no created intermediary. Of course, Athanasius shares with his opponents the biblical teaching that God creates through the Logos. But he does not see the Word as a created intermediary, but as the very presence of God to creatures, as the uncreated Word who comes down to creatures, who "condescends" to be with creatures in self-humbling love. Referring to the Colossians hymn that proclaims Christ as the "firstborn of creation" (1:15), Athanasius writes:

> For it is clear to all that he was called the "firstborn" of creation not as being of himself a creature nor because of any kinship of essence with all creation, but because the Word condescended [*sunkatabebēke*] to the things coming into being when he was creating them at the beginning so that they be enabled to come into being. For they would not have withstood his nature, being that of the unmitigated splendor of the Father, if he had not condescended [*sunkatabas*] by the Father's love for humanity and supported, strengthened, and carried them into being.[45]

---

[44] Peter Leithart, *Athanasius* (Grand Rapids, MI: Baker Academic, 2011), 91.

[45] Athanasius, *Orations against the Arians*, 2.64, in Anatolios, *Athanasius*, 157–58.

In creation and incarnation, the Word of God who is radically beyond all creatures condescends to be directly present to creatures out of generous, compassionate, loving-kindness. Anatolios points out that Athanasius transforms the idea of divine transcendence by means of the biblical categories of divine mercy and loving-kindness. In creation and incarnation, there is a "simultaneous contrast and interplay" between two attributes of God, God as "beyond all being [*hyperekeina pasēs ousias*]"[46] and God's "goodness and loving-kindness [*philanthrōpia*]."[47] Because of the divine attribute of loving-kindness, Anatolios notes, God can transcend God's own transcendence:

> Characterizing God primarily in terms of *philanthrōpia* and mercy—attributes whereby God can transcend his own transcendence—explains why no mediated being is needed and how the incarnation accords with the character of God's being and the divine deportment in the creation.[48]

Athanasius is thus engaged in a "reconstructing" of divine transcendence.[49] Instead of associating transcendence with the Father, and immanence with the Logos, like his opponents, Athanasius understands both attributes as belonging to the divine being as such, and harmonizes them through the notion of *philanthrōpia*. Perhaps it can be said that the true nature of divine transcendence, characterized as an unthinkable divine capacity for *philanthrōpia*, is far beyond inadequate human notions of transcendence, which might seem to limit God to a

---

[46] Athanasius, *Against the Greeks* 2.

[47] Anatolios, *Athanasius*, 40.

[48] Khaled Anatolios, *Retrieving Nicaea: The Development and Meaning of Trinitarian Doctrine* (Grand Rapids, MI: Baker Academic, 2011), 104.

[49] Ibid.

realm apart from creation. An inadequate and human concept of transcendence can be used to put limits on God's capacity to be present in love with God's creatures in creation and incarnation. What Athanasius transcends, then, is a limited, finite view of divine transcendence, with his insistence on the generous loving kindness of God.

Anatolios points out, in the quotation above, that for Athanasius the character of God in creating is in full accord with the kenotic character of God revealed in the incarnation. In both creation and incarnation, the Word of God is a self-humbling God, who descends to be with creatures, for the sake of their creation and deification. Commenting on Philippians 2:5–11, Athanasius completely rejects his opponents' view that Jesus Christ was first a creature and then advanced to divine status. On the contrary, he insists, the Word was always God, and in taking flesh and accepting death on a cross "he was not advanced but rather humbled himself."[50] For Athanasius, then, Christ is "the descending, self-humbling God."[51] This divine self-humbling is for the sake of our advancement, that we might be deified as God's sons and daughters.

In Athanasius's theology of incarnation, the self-humbling of the Savior is not simply to be located in the humanity of Jesus, but is rather the true expression of the divine nature. God's self-humbling in creation and incarnation springs from the love of the triune God and belongs to the divine nature itself. Anatolios writes: "In Athanasius's account, a divine self-abasement is integral to the biblical character of God; this divine humility belongs to the divine nature directly, rather than to a separate mediating being, and enables direct contact between the transcendent God and his creation."[52]

Because Word and Spirit are one with the Father in essence, their creative presence to creatures means that the Father, the

---

[50] Athanasius, *Against the Arians*, 1.39–40.

[51] Anatolios, *Retrieving Nicaea*, 123.

[52] Ibid., 119.

Source of All, is also immediately present to each creature.[53] As Athanasius puts it, using a favorite trinitarian image, the one who experiences the Radiance is enlightened by the Sun itself and not by any intermediary.[54] A fully trinitarian theology of God enables us to glimpse the immediacy of the relationship between God and God's creatures. Every creature on earth, every whale, every sparrow, exists by participation in the Source of All through the Word in the Spirit—"not one of them is forgotten in God's sight" (Lk 12:6).

Anatolios points to the way that Athanasius's Christological redefinition of the divine nature as self-humbling in love is taken further in Gregory of Nyssa. In his *Catechetical Orations*, Gregory asks how the humiliation of the cross is congruent with the majesty of the divine nature: "Why, then, they ask, did the divine stoop to such humiliation? Our faith falters when we think that God, the infinite, the incomprehensible, ineffable reality, transcending all glory and majesty, should be defiled by associating with human nature, and his sublime powers no less debased by their contact with what is abject."[55] In response, Gregory takes up the Athanasian notion of *philanthrōpia* and presents it as the proper mark of the divine nature.[56] He goes further in reconstructing the notion of divine transcendence. Divine transcendence should not be construed negatively as God's incapacity to engage directly with creatures. Rather, Gregory proposes that the supreme example of divine power is the loving self-abasement of God in choosing to share the human condition in the incarnation:

> In the first place, that the omnipotent nature was capable of descending to the human's lowly position is

---

[53] Anatolios, *Athanasius: The Coherence of His Thought*, 113.

[54] Athanasius, *Against the Arians*, 3.14.

[55] Gregory of Nyssa, *Catechetical Orations* 14, in Anatolios, *Retrieving Nicaea*, 203.

[56] Ibid.

clearer evidence of power than great and supernatural miracles. For it somehow accords with God's nature and is consistent with it, to do great and sublime things by divine power. It does not startle us to hear it said that the whole creation, including the invisible world, exists by God's power, and is the realization of his will. But descent to the human's lowly position is a supreme example of power, a power that is not bounded by circumstances contrary to its nature. . . . God's transcendent power is not so much displayed in the vastness of the universe, or the luster of the stars, or the orderly arrangement of the universe or his perpetual oversight of it, as in his condescension to our weak nature. We marvel at the way Godhead was entwined in human nature, and in becoming human, did not cease to be God.[57]

Gregory redefines divine power in terms of the loving self-abasement of God in the incarnation. God's self-abasement, then, is not the opposite of divine power, but the radical expression of the *philanthrōpia* of the divine nature in our history. It is the supreme expression of divine power. I think, then, that Paul Gavrilyuk is right to say that the notion of impassibility functions as "a kind of apophatic qualifier of all divine emotions and as the marker of the unmistakably divine identity."[58] It defends the radical transcendence of God, and when applied to Word and Spirit, their full and equal divinity. What it rules out are fickleness, arbitrariness, and inconstancy, and all the emotions and passions unworthy of God that are found in mythological gods, including lust, jealousy, vengeance, and violence. It does not rule out the God-befitting

---

[57] Ibid.

[58] Paul L. Gavrilyuk, *The Suffering of the Impassible God: The Dialectics of Patristic Thought* (Oxford: Oxford University Press, 2006), 173.

emotions, proclaimed in the Scriptures, such as love, compassion, and generosity, when it is acknowledged that they are of Godlike kind, infinitely beyond all human emotions.

Athanasius and Deep Incarnation: Critical Differences, Resonances, and Insights

As with Irenaeus, there are obvious differences between Athanasius's incarnational theology and contemporary theologies of deep incarnation, as well as resonances and insights from Athanasius that can be foundational for a contemporary theology of deep incarnation. Differences are inevitable because of the dissimilarity of contexts and issues addressed. Athanasius was responding to questions about the eternity and divinity of the Word, which he saw as endangering the Christian understanding of the saving incarnation, while deep incarnation is concerned with the meaning of salvation for the wider creation, and with the suffering and loss involved in an evolutionary world.

Critical Differences

- Athanasius never had to confront today's ecological crisis, and so does not often focus his attention directly on the wider creation. His focus is on the full divinity of the Word who becomes incarnate and its meaning for the deifying transformation of humanity. But he sees the creative Word as lovingly present to all creatures, and includes the wider creation in salvation in Christ.
- He does not share our contemporary evolutionary consciousness that heightens the theological problem of the suffering of nonhuman as well as human creatures. He does not speak of the Word as suffering with suffering creation in the way that is proposed in the theology of deep incarnation.

Resonances and Foundational Insights

- The Word is present as Creator to all creatures, "bringing into existence," "governing," "establishing," "leading," "providing for," and "ordering" creation. Each creature "*participates* in the Word who is truly from the Father," and the Word "gives life and protection to everything, everywhere, to each individually and to all together."[59]

- The Word of Creation is the Word on the Cross. Creation and incarnation are profoundly linked in a theology of the Word and the Spirit: The Father creates and renews all things through the Word in the Spirit.

- Although the incarnation of the Word is radically unique to Jesus Christ, it is an event that is transformative and deifying for all other creatures: "For he became human that we might become divine"; Christ, "the Liberator of all flesh and of all creation (cf. Rom. 8:21)."[60]

- The incarnation, and above all the cross, witness to the kenotic and self-humbling nature of God. The theological understanding of the divine nature of the God who creates is determined by Christology, and particularly by the cross.

- The wider creaturely world is explicitly and unambiguously included in the eschatological transformation and deification of all things in Christ. Athanasius sees the whole creation as participating in the cross and in life-giving resurrection.

- Divine transcendence is reconstructed in terms of the biblical notions of God's descending, self-humbling love. This self-humbling, which is characteristic of God's action in creation and salvation, belongs to the

---

[59] Athanasius, *Against the Greeks*, 41,

[60] Athanasius, *On the Incarnation*, 54; *To Adelphius*, 4, in Anatolios, *Athanasius*, 238.

divine nature itself. Gregory of Nyssa redefines divine power in terms of the loving self-abasement of God in the incarnation. The self-humbling love of the incarnation, then, is not the opposite of divine power, but the true expression of divine power. Athanasius's theology does not support the idea of an impassive, unfeeling, and distant God. It opens space for a contemporary theology to affirm both divine transcendence and God's transcendent capacity to feel with, and in some way to suffer with, suffering creation.

- If the kenotic love of the cross is the very love that is at work in the creation, then in the light of modern science it can be said, with the theologians of deep incarnation, that it is this kenotic and self-humbling love that is at work in the emergence of the universe over the last 13.7 billion years, and the evolution of life on earth over the last 3.7 billion years, with all its terrible costs and in all its wonderful outcomes. It can offer support for the claim that God is compassionately present to all the creatures of our evolutionary world, accompanying creatures in their groaning, and promising them their participation in the liberation and fulfillment of all things in Christ.

4

Karl Rahner on Incarnation in an Evolutionary World

Karl Rahner (1904–1984) is rightly thought of as a theologian of grace. In his theology, every human being, at every point in time, exists within a situation of God's free self-offering love. Grace, for him, is primarily uncreated grace, which is God present in the Spirit. Grace is God, freely giving God's self in love to all who accept this divine self-offering. We are born into, and live in, a world of grace. But if Rahner is a theologian of grace, he is equally a theologian of the incarnation. Grace is always the saving and life-giving grace of the Word made flesh. It is only through the revelation given in Christ that we can know surely that the mystery and transcendence we experience in our everyday lives is the place of encounter with a loving and gracious God. In Rahner's thought, the grace of the Spirit and the incarnation of the Word are radically interrelated and cannot be separated.[1]

---

[1] I will be referring particularly to Karl Rahner, *Theological Investigations*, 23 vols. (hereafter *TI*), trans. various (Baltimore: Helicon Press, and New York: Crossroad, 1962–92); to Karl Rahner et al., eds., *Sacramentum Mundi: An Encyclopedia of Theology* (hereafter *SM*), 6 vols. (New York: Herder and Herder, 1968); and to Rahner's *Foundations of Christian Faith: An Introduction to the Idea of Christianity* (hereafter *Foundations*), trans. William V. Dych (New York: Crossroad, 1978).

A fundamental structuring concept in Rahner's theology is that of God's self-giving, or self-bestowal. This is a fully trinitarian concept: God (the Father) gives God's self to us in Jesus the Word made flesh, and in the Spirit poured out in grace. The great truths of Christian faith, the incarnation, the grace of the Spirit, and the Trinity, are summed up in the concept of God bestowing God's self to us in the Word and the Spirit. This divine self-giving begins in creation itself, and reaches its unthinkable depths in the incarnation. Creation and incarnation are linked together as distinct aspects of God's free decision to give God's self in love to a world of creatures.[2]

Rahner's thought on the incarnation is never developed in a fully systematic way. Roman Siebenrock shows how Rahner's work on Christology emerges over three periods of his life, as he takes up and explores a large number of specific Christological issues.[3] In this chapter I take up just five aspects of Rahner's theology that I see as important in the contemporary discussion of deep incarnation: (1) the unchanging God as changing in the incarnation; (2) the deep reach of the incarnation and the cross; (3) incarnation in an evolutionary theology; (4) resurrection as involving the whole creation; and (5) incarnation in relation to extraterrestrial life. In the final chapter I will return to Rahner and build on his notion of a symbolic/sacramental understanding of the redemption.

The Unchanging God Changes in the Incarnation

Karl Rahner accepts the long-standing Christian tradition that God is a God of infinite fullness, who is rightly understood as constant and unchanging, as pure act (*actus purus*). But he

---

[2] Rahner, *Foundations*, 197.

[3] Roman Siebenrock, "Christology," in *The Cambridge Companion to Karl Rahner*, ed. Declan Marmion and Mary E. Hines (Cambridge: Cambridge University Press, 2005), 112–27.

asks how this concept can be related to the central Christian doctrine that, in the incarnation, the Word *became* flesh. What does it mean for the eternal Word of God to *become*? Can God *become* anything?

Rahner rejects the view that in the incarnation change occurs only in the creaturely humanity of Jesus, not in the eternal Word of God. He says that the result of this position would be that "all change and history, with all their tribulation, remain on this side of the absolute gulf which necessarily sunders the unchangeable God from the world of change and prevents them from mingling."[4] He finds this view inadequate because it fails to show that what happened to Jesus is precisely the history of the very Word of God. He sees the Christian tradition as involving the claim that it is truly the eternal Word of God who undergoes the events of Jesus's life and his death.

Rahner's own position is that God, who is unchangeable in God's self, can change in another, in becoming a creature, in becoming human. The infinite God, who is pure freedom, possesses the possibility to become what is other, the finite. In Rahner's view of the incarnation, it is not simply that God assumes a preexisting creature, but that God gives Godself to the other, and in so doing poses the other as God's own reality. What is fundamental, then, to the Christian view of the incarnation, Rahner says, is "the *self*-emptying, the coming to be, the κένωσις and γένεσις of God himself, who can come to be by becoming another thing."[5] So Rahner insists, like Athanasius, on the paradox that God is not only immutable but can also truly become something. I think Rahner makes an important claim, one that has significance for deep incarnation, when he says that the dialectical possibility of the unchanging God becoming a creature does not represent a deficiency in

---

[4] Karl Rahner, "On the Theology of the Incarnation," *TI*, 4:105–120, at 113.

[5] Ibid., 114.

God but, rather, the fullness of God. God would be less if God could *not* become other. God's transcendence, understood in the light of the incarnation, should not be thought of as limiting God's freedom to become a creature. Rather, a true understanding of divine transcendence would acknowledge God's freedom to give God's self in self-emptying love into the finite other. God has the possibility of freely subjecting God's self to history.

At the heart of all this, Rahner points out, is the radical nature of divine love. God who is the fullness of love, and who remains in this fullness, can also pour out this love, in self-emptying self-bestowal. This kenotic love can constitute the finite other as God's own proper reality. God goes out of God's self, in love that gives itself away. This, Rahner says, is the meaning of the scriptural definition of God as love.[6] God is the fullness of love, and always remains the fullness of love, but this love is of such a kind that it can involve the freely chosen, kenotic giving of self to a world of creatures. Prodigal freedom and love is who God is. This line of thought is highly significant for deep incarnation, because what Rahner says of God's transcendence finding its true expression in the kenotic love of the incarnation can also be applied to the divine act of creation. Creation is intrinsically directed to the incarnation, and it, too, can be understood as an inner part of God's act of self-giving and kenotic love toward creatures.

The Deep Reach of the Incarnation and the Cross

An often quoted saying of Christian theology appears in a letter written by Gregory Nazianzus (329–390): "What has not been assumed has not been healed."[7] Gregory was comment-

---

6 Ibid., 115.

7 Gregory Nazianzus, *Epistle* 101, trans. Lionel Wickham, in "The First Letter to Cledonius the Presbyter," in *On God and Christ: St. Greg-*

ing on the theology of Apollinaris (310–390), who had denied the human rational mind in Christ. Gregory insists that in the incarnation the Word assumes not just a human body, but also a human mind and soul. His argument is that if the whole of the human is to be saved and transformed in Christ, then the incarnation must involve the Word assuming all that makes up the human. Karl Rahner takes up and extends Gregory's saying to outline his own position that, in the incarnation, *all of creaturely reality* is assumed, so that the whole universe of creatures might participate in salvation:

> If anything was not assumed, neither was it redeemed. . . . But *everything* has been assumed, for Christ is true human being, true son of Adam, truly lived a human life in all its breadth and height and depth. And hence, everything, without confusion and without separation, is to enter into eternal life; there is to be not only a new heaven but a new earth. Nothing, unless it be eternally damned, can remain outside the blessing, the protection, the transfiguration of this divinization of the whole, which, beginning in Christ, aims at drawing everything that exists into the life of God himself, precisely in order that it may thus have eternal validity conferred upon it. This is the reality of Christ, which constitutes Christianity, the incarnate life of God in our place and our time.[8]

In this text Rahner comes close to a contemporary theology of deep incarnation, not only in his use of spatial metaphors,

---

ory of *Nazianzus: The Five Theological Orations and Two Letters to Cledonius* (Crestwood, NY: St. Vladimir's Seminary Press, 2002), 155–66, at 158.

[8] Karl Rahner, *Mission and Grace: Essays in Pastoral Theology II* (London: Sheed and Ward, 1963), 39–42. Roman Siebenrock uses this as the epigraph for his chapter "Christology," in *The Cambridge Companion*, 112.

when he says that Christ lived a human life in all its breadth and height and depth, but also, more importantly, in his insistence that in Christ all is assumed, so that all is saved, all is to be transfigured, all is to be brought into the life of God, all is to participate in deification. The only exception to the universal reach of the transfiguration of all things in Christ is found in those who freely reject it—Rahner insists that we must keep open the possibility that humans may freely choose to reject God radically and eternally, but he also believes that we may hope that in the end all will be saved.

A further reflection on the depth and breadth of the incarnation is found in Rahner's meditation from 1950 titled "A Faith That Loves the Earth."[9] In this text he insists that we human beings are truly of the earth, that earth is our mother, and that our destiny is to be found not in our spirits escaping to some distant land of God's glory, but in the bodily world we inhabit. The earth is our permanent home, yet the earth itself suffers from impermanence, pain, and death. Rahner comments that the earth gives birth to children of immense appetites, "and what she gives them is too beautiful to be ignored by them and too little to ever satisfy them."[10] We children of the earth long for more, for fullness of life.

In this context Rahner ponders the message of Jesus's death and resurrection. He insists that Jesus's death was not an escape to another world, but an entry into the depth of the earth. In his death, Jesus descends into the heart of created reality. Rahner points to the words of Jesus in Matthew 12:40: "For three days and three nights the Son of Man will be in the heart of the earth." In his meditation on this text, Rahner sees it as suggesting that Jesus will go down "to the heart of all earthly things, where everything is interconnected and one,

---

[9] Karl Rahner, "A Faith That Loves the Earth," in *The Mystical Way in Everyday Life: Sermons: Essays and Prayers: Karl Rahner, SJ*, ed. Annemarie S. Kidder (Maryknoll, NY: Orbis Books, 2010), 52–58.

[10] Ibid., 53.

to the seat of death and earth's impermanence."[11] In his death, Jesus enters into the very heart of the earth in order to infuse it with divine life:

> In his death, the Lord descended into the lowest and deepest regions of what is visible. It is no longer a place of impermanence and death, because there *he* now is. By his death, he has become the heart of this earthly world, God's heart in the center of the world, where the world even before its own unfolding in space and time taps into God's power and might.[12]

Christ dies, Rahner seems to be saying, into the heart of the earth, and also into God's creative act that is enabling and empowering the whole universe. The Word made flesh becomes in a new interior way "God's heart" at the very center of creation. And his resurrection is not to be seen as an abandonment of the earth and its creatures. Because he is raised precisely in the body, he remains profoundly connected to all that is bodily:

> No, he is risen in his body. That means: He has begun to transfigure this world into himself; he has accepted this world forever; he has been born anew as a child of this earth, but of an earth that is transfigured, freed, unlimited, an earth that in him will last forever and is delivered from death and impermanence for good.[13]

The risen Christ is still part of the earth, deeply connected to the earth's nature and destiny: "By rising he has not left the dwelling of the earth, since he still has his body, though in a final and transfigured way, and is part of the earth, a part that

---

[11] Ibid., 54.
[12] Ibid., 55.
[13] Ibid.

still belongs to the earth, and is connected with earth's nature and destiny."[14] Despite the ongoing struggle and the pain of life, at the very heart of earth something radically new has begun. The forces of a transfigured world are already at work in the risen Christ, conquering impermanence, death, and sin at their core. Although we continue to experience suffering and sin in the world, Christian faith holds that they have actually been defeated deep down at their very source: "His resurrection is like the first erupting of a volcano, which shows that the fire of God is already burning inside the world and its light will eventually bring everything else to a blessed glow."[15] The new forces of transfiguration are already at work, because the risen Christ does not abandon us or the earth, but is radically present to creatures in their longing:

> Christ is already at the very heart of all the lowly things of the earth that we are unable to let go of and that belong to the earth as mother. He is at the heart of the nameless yearning of all creatures, waiting—though perhaps unaware that they are waiting—to be allowed to participate in the transfiguration of his body. He is at the heart of earth's history, whose blind progress amidst all victories and defeats is headed with uncanny precision toward the day that is his, where his glory will break forth from its own depths, thereby transforming everything. He is at the heart of all tears and all death as concealed rejoicing and as the life that gains victory by its apparent death. He is at the heart of one's handing something to a beggar as the secret wealth that is bestowed on the beggar.[16]

---

14. Ibid.
15. Ibid., 56.
16. Ibid., 56–57.

The risen Christ, Rahner says, is "the heart of this earthly world and the secret seal of its everlasting promise."[17] Earth is our mother, and we are children of the earth, and we are called to love the earth. We do not need to think of ourselves as leaving the earth for God, because God's life is in it. The earth is, or will become, the body of the risen one. Our call is to love the earth and to love God together, "for in the resurrection of the Lord, God has shown that he has adopted the earth forever."[18] God has come to us in the flesh in Jesus's life, death, and resurrection and, since that time, "Mother Earth has brought forth only creatures that will be transfigured, for his resurrection is the beginning of the resurrection of all flesh."[19] Even though Rahner seldom speaks explicitly of animal and plants, it is notable that he includes all the creatures brought forth by Mother Earth in this promised transfiguration.

Incarnation in an Evolutionary World

Throughout his theological career, Rahner saw the need to understand the incarnation in fresh ways in light of the new picture of reality that was emerging from scientific cosmology and evolutionary biology.[20] He points out that whereas traditional theology assumed a static world, we can now see that there have been massive transitions in the history of the universe, including the transitions from matter to the first forms of life on earth, and the transition from early forms of life to various species of *homo*, and to modern humans, with their extremely complex brains. This leads Rahner to ask: How should we think about the incarnation in the light of an evolutionary view of the world in which we live?

---

[17] Ibid., 57.

[18] Ibid., 58.

[19] Ibid.

[20] See, for example, "Christology within an Evolutionary View of the World," *TI*, 6:157–92.

Rahner makes two fundamental assumptions in responding to this question. The first is that humans belong in one interconnected world, existing only in evolutionary and ecological interrelation with the biological and material world in which they evolve. The human spirit, with its unique consciousness and freedom, emerges only as radically related to matter. So Rahner speaks of biologically organized matter as "oriented in terms of an ever-increasing complexity and interiority towards spirit."[21] Under the impulse of God's creative Spirit, matter comes to transcend itself and becomes self-conscious spirit. In Rahner's view, the unity of the one universe, and the unity of matter and spirit, have direct significance for Christology. A radical unity of this kind supports the understanding that the incarnation involves a hypostatic union of the Logos, not just with the isolated humanity of Jesus, but with the matter of the universe as such, with the radical potentiality of the whole creation. Such a unity of the one world of matter, flesh, and consciousness shows, Rahner says, "why the total reality of the world is *ipso facto* touched to its very roots by the incarnation of the Logos precisely in virtue of the fact that matter must be must be conceived of fundamentally and from the outset as one."[22]

A second fundamental assumption for Rahner is that, whereas many theologians have seen the reason for the incarnation simply as the salvation of sinful humanity, he holds to the tradition associated with Duns Scotus (c. 1266–1308), but also with many others, that from the very beginning God's creation is directed to the incarnation. Irrespective of human sin, the divine intention in creating a world of creatures was always freely to give God's self to creatures in the incarnation, and so to bring them to their fulfillment.[23] God creates

---

[21] Karl Rahner, "Christology in the Setting of Modern Man's Understanding of Himself and of His World," *TI*, 11:215–29, at 218.

[22] Ibid., 219.

[23] Ibid.

a world in order to give God's self to creatures in the Word made flesh and in the Spirit poured out. Harvey Egan writes that the briefest summary of Rahner's theology is "his creative appropriation of Scotus' view that God creates in order to communicate *self* and that creation exists in order to be the recipient of God's free gift of self."[24]

The creation of a world of creatures is, from the outset, an element in God's will to impart God's self to that which was not divine: "This world constitutes in a very radical sense the environment, the concomitant setting, indeed the very physicality demanded by the Logos in its act of uttering itself into the non-divine."[25] This means that God's self-bestowal in incarnation and grace is not a subsequent addition to creation:

> On the contrary, the creation, considered as the constitution of the non-divine "out of nothing," is revealed as the prior setting and condition for the supreme possibility of his imparting of himself "to the outside world" to be realized, a self-bestowal in which he does not constitute some other being, different from himself, but imparts himself, and thereby effectively manifests himself as the *agape* that bestows itself.[26]

Rahner points out that, although Christianity has always had the concept of saving history, until recently it has been understood as played out on the stage of a static material and biological world. God was seen as profoundly present to creatures, conserving them in being (the concept of *conservatio*) and collaborating with them in their activities (the concept of *concursus*). Rahner's contribution is to propose that God's creative presence to creatures enables creation itself to produce

---

24 Harvey D. Egan, "Theology and Spirituality," in *The Cambridge Companion*, 13–28, at 16.

25 Rahner, "Christology in the Setting," 220.

26 Ibid.

essentially new entities. In this view, God's creative presence enables a genuine becoming in the creaturely world, in a process that Rahner calls *self-transcendence*.[27] Whereas the theology of the past saw the immanent presence and power of God as "conserving and maintaining the abiding order of things," our evolutionary consciousness requires a theology that shows "the immanence of the divine dynamism in the world as a becoming."[28] The *self* in self-transcendence is meant to indicate that this capacity comes from within creaturely reality. In the relationship of creation, God gives to creatures themselves the capacity to cross thresholds into the new. God bestows on the world its own capacity for creativity and novelty. The divine creative presence, then, is understood as empowering the becoming of the world.

It is precisely God's self-bestowal in Word and Spirit that enables creaturely self-transcendence. Rahner's insight transforms the classical theology of creation and enables it to function in a new, evolutionary era. This insight offers new, deeper insight into God, as a Creator who delights in participation, and in the emergence of creaturely reality through increasing complexity. When this process is understood from the perspective of its culmination in the grace of the Spirit and the incarnation of the Word, then it can be seen that, in this whole unified history, God gives God's very self to creatures. This means, for Rahner, that "the reality of God himself is imparted to the world as its supreme specification." This self-giving by which God becomes constitutive of creatures without compromising divine transcendence, Rahner calls *quasi-formal causality*.[29]

The theology of self-transcendence is a fundamental structural link between Rahner's theology of creation and his evo-

---

[27] See, for example, Karl Rahner, *Foundations*, 183–87; "Evolution," in *Encyclopedia of Theology: A Concise Sacramentum Mundi*, ed. Karl Rahner (London: Burns and Oates, 1975), 478–84.

[28] Rahner, "Christology in the Setting," 219.

[29] Ibid., 225.

lutionary Christology.[30] The divine act of self-giving love by which God creates a world of creatures through creaturely self-transcendence is always centered on the incarnation.[31] The incarnation, then, is not only the culmination of God's self-bestowal to creatures but also the culmination of the self-transcendence of creatures to God.

Jesus is, in his humanity, like all of us, a product of biological evolution. But unlike us, Jesus can be seen as the unique and unforeseeable culmination of the process of self-transcendence, of matter to life, and of life to self-conscious humanity, and of self-conscious creatures to God. Rahner sees the universe as borne from its very beginning by a thrust toward a dynamic and conscious relationship with its Creator. The goal of the universe is God's communication with it. Jesus is the creature who responds to God with radical love, the love poured out in his life and ministry, which finds ultimate expression in the cross. From the perspective of his humanity, then, Jesus is the unique self-transcendence of creation to God.

From the perspective of his divinity, Jesus is the unique, irreversible culmination of God's self-bestowal to a world of creatures. For Rahner, then, Jesus is the "absolute savior" because he is both God's irrevocable self-giving to creation, and in his human life and death, the radical response of creation to God.[32] He is both God's forgiving, healing, liberating

---

[30] Rahner employs this concept in his theology of the creation of the human soul. See his *Hominisation: The Evolutionary Origin of Man as a Theological Problem* (New York: Herder and Herder, 1968); "Evolution," in *Encyclopedia of Theology*, 478–88. He also makes use of it in his understanding of eschatology. See his "Immanent and Transcendent Consummation of the World," *TI*, 10:273–92; "A Fragmentary Aspect of the Theological Evaluation of the Concept of the Future," *TI*, 10:235–41; and "The Theological Problems Entailed in the Idea of the 'New Earth,'" *TI*, 10:260–72.

[31] See Rahner, *Foundations*, 178–203; "Christology within an Evolutionary View of the World," *TI*, 5:157–92.

[32] Rahner, *Foundations*, 195.

embrace of creation in self-giving love and creation's unreserved "yes!" to God. The incarnate Word is both the irrevocable self-bestowal of God to a world of creatures and the definitive creaturely acceptance of this self-bestowal.

In the resurrection and the ascension of the risen Christ, the creaturely reality of Jesus is taken fully into God, and irrevocably adopted as God's own reality, as the beginning and the pledge of the transfiguration of the whole creation. Rahner sees the first and second coming of the incarnate Word as a unity,

> a single event still in the process of achieving its fullness, such that in it the life, death and resurrection of Jesus constitute merely the first beginning of an event which will only have achieved its fullness and definitive state when the world as a whole is illumined by, and brought face to face with, the immediacy of God, and in this sense when Jesus himself will have "come again."[33]

This is interconnected with a second theological position about the body of Christ: Christ can be understood rightly only if he, as the head and the body, which is the church and ultimately the whole created world itself, are grasped as constituting the one and whole Christ.[34]

Resurrection and the Transfiguration of the Whole Universe

In an article written in the 1950s exploring the meaning of the resurrection, Rahner points out that Western theology, with its juridical notion of the redemption, had tended to focus on the cross as offering satisfaction for human sin, while almost com-

---

[33] Rahner, "Christology in the Setting," 228.
[34] Ibid.

pletely ignoring the resurrection.[35] In the East, Rahner writes, the whole event of Jesus Christ, the life, death, and resurrection, is understood as being not only about the forgiveness of sin, but also about overcoming death and enabling participation in God. It involves the transformation of human beings and, with them, of the whole creation, so that the redemption begun in the incarnation is seen as involving the "divinization of the world."[36]

Rahner sees the death of Jesus as the final act by which the whole of his life, lived in love and obedience to God, is gathered up in freedom. It is not simply one act among others, but the "totality of Christ in act, the definitive act of his freedom, the complete integration of his time on earth with his human eternity."[37] The resurrection is not only an event that occurs after Jesus's death, but is the manifestation of what happens in his death, as he hands his whole bodily existence into the mystery of a loving God, and is fully received by this God. In the cross of Jesus, part of this world freely and radically gives itself to God in complete love and obedience and is fully taken up into God. Rahner sees this event as salvific and transformative for the whole of creation: "This is Easter, and the redemption of the world."[38]

In the resurrection of Jesus, God essentially and irrevocably adopts creaturely reality as God's own reality. This occurs by God's primordial act, which finds expression in the incarnation of the Word, and the life and death of Jesus culminating in the resurrection that transfigures the creaturely reality of Jesus. Because of the unity of the world that springs from God in the one divine economy, Rahner says, this transfiguration of the crucified Jesus is an event for the whole world. What occurs in Jesus, as part of a physical, biological, and human world, is

---

[35] Rahner, "Dogmatic Questions on Easter," *TI*, 4:121–33.

[36] Ibid., 126.

[37] Ibid., 128.

[38] Ibid.

ontologically and not just juridically "the embryonically final beginning of the glorification and divinization of the whole of reality."[39]

In a world in which creation and saving incarnation are radically united as aspects of the one divine act of self-bestowal, the resurrection can be understood as the irreversible beginning of the fulfillment of God's will in creating a universe of creatures. Rahner sees it as "the beginning of the transformation of the world as an ontologically interconnected occurrence."[40] He speaks of the risen Christ as the "pledge and beginning of the perfect fulfillment of the world" and as the "representative of the new cosmos."[41] The risen Christ is already at work in the whole universe as both the pledge and the reality of its future. As the risen one, Christ is freed from "the limiting individuality of the unglorified body" and in his glorified new state is already present to all of creation.[42] What we think of as his second coming in glory, then, will be the clear revelation of his transforming engagement with creatures that is already occurring: it will be "the disclosure of this relation to the world attained by Jesus in his resurrection."[43]

In Rahner's view, contemporary cosmology is a help to theologians in thinking about the final state of the universe. In earlier times, when the universe was thought of as a series of spheres, eternal life could be imagined as moving from the everyday sphere to a heavenly sphere. But with the current scientific picture of an evolving universe, we are better able to think about a God-given final state of the universe as a whole. Rahner recognizes, however, that there is no easy transition from the dismal scientific predictions of the end of earth, and of the final state of the universe as a whole, to a Christian

---

[39] Ibid., 129.

[40] Rahner, "Resurrection," in *Encyclopedia of Theology*, 1438–42.

[41] Ibid., 1442.

[42] Ibid.

[43] Ibid.

eschatology. In his view, the fulfillment of the universe can happen only through a transformative act of God, but he also insists that we are called to be part of this. Our contributions, our commitments to justice and peace, our acts of love, our prayer, our small acts of fidelity, will be taken up in new creation. This new creation will be God's act, but it will involve the self-transcendence of our own commitment to others, to the poor of the earth, and to the planetary community of life.[44]

Rahner sees the Second Coming of Christ as involving not only human beings but also the whole world of creatures of which they are a part. It will not take place for humans in an unchanged world, but will involve a radical transformation of the whole of reality. The universe will reach its fulfillment by participating in the reality already possessed by the risen Christ: "The world as a whole flows into his Resurrection and into the transfiguration of his body," so that Christ "will be revealed to all reality and, within it, to every one of its parts in its own way, as the innermost secret of all the world and of all history."[45]

Although Rahner holds that the bodily resurrection of humans and the transformation of the universe must be understood together, he is convinced that they are both beyond our imagining and comprehension, because our future, and that of the universe, is in the incomprehensible mystery of God. What we have is not a clear picture, but an unbreakable promise of God in the resurrection of the crucified Christ. In Christ, resurrection is revealed to be not the revival of a corpse, but radical transformation (1 Cor 15:44). In the God-given transformation of the universe, Rahner says, "It will then be equally correct to call the new reality a new heaven or a new earth."[46]

---

[44] See the articles on eschatology referred to in footnote 30 above.

[45] Karl Rahner, "The Resurrection of the Body," *TI*, 2:203–216, at 213.

46 Ibid., 215.

Because Rahner sees the matter of the universe not as disappearing, but as reaching its true fulfillment in Christ, he says that Christians thus have, or should have, a very high regard for matter. Christians are the true materialists: they are really "the most sublime of materialists . . . more crassly materialist than those who call themselves so."[47] It is true that the matter of the universe will also undergo a radical transformation, "the depths of which we can only sense with fear and trembling in that process which we experience as our death."[48] But because of their convictions about resurrection and ascension, Rahner sees Christians as committed to the idea that matter will last forever, and be glorified forever in Christ. This transfiguration of the matter of the world has already begun in Christ, and is already "ripening and developing to that point where it will become manifest."[49]

Extraterrestrials

Rahner's thought about the natural world was usually focused on our home planet, but he also reflects on what astronomy and cosmology tell us about the size of the universe and the billions of galaxies in the observable universe, that can lead to a sense of "cosmic dizziness." Of course he would be made even dizzier by the very recent estimates, based on data from the Hubble telescope, that there may be two trillion galaxies in the observable universe, and by cosmologists talking of the possibility of multiverses. Rahner speaks of cosmic dizziness as an element in the development of our theological and religious consciousness. It can bring to awareness what he sees as primary theological datum, the incomprehensible mystery of God: the unimaginable size of the universe is "to a certain extent, nothing other than the spatial counterpart to the theo-

---

[47] Rahner, "The Festival of the Future of the World," *TI*, 7:181–85.
[48] Ibid., 183.
[49] Ibid., 184.

logical datum" of God's radically incomprehensible mystery.[50] Experience of such a universe, he suggests, can lead to a deeply religious sense of our human contingency and creatureliness.

Although astronomers had long believed that planets must exist around stars other than our sun, the first exoplanet was discovered only in 1992. Since then, more and more have been found. Many of them are gas giants, like Jupiter, and only a small percentage appear to resemble earth in its hospitality to life, but it is natural in this context to ask about the possibility of extraterrestrial life and its meaning for theology. In addition, the recent discoveries of extremophiles, microbial forms of life that can flourish in niches that are acidic or extremely hot or cold, have made us aware that we need to radically expand our view of the places in the universe where life might exist. The question of extraterrestrial life is a live one for many of our contemporaries.

This is not a new question, but one that has been addressed by philosophers and theologians throughout the ages, including Thomas O'Meara quite recently.[51] Rahner has made brief comments on this issue several times, in an early encyclopedia article on "star-dwellers," and later in his article on "Natural Science and Reasonable Faith," in volume 21 of his *Theological Investigations*, and a few paragraphs in his *Foundations of Christian Faith*.[52] In Rahner's view, Christian theology cannot

---

[50] Karl Rahner, "Natural Science and Reasonable Faith," *TI*, 21:16–55, at 50.

[51] Thomas O'Meara, *Vast Universe: Extraterrestrials and Christian Revelation* (Collegeville, MN: Liturgical, 2012). See Michael Crowe, *The Extraterrestrial Debate, 1750–1900* (Cambridge: Cambridge University Press, 1986); *The Extraterrestrial Debate, Antiquity to 1915* (Notre Dame: University of Notre Dame Press, 2008). See also Steven Dick, ed., *Many Worlds: The New Universe, Extraterrestrial Life and the Theological Implications* (Philadelphia: Templeton Foundation, 2000); and David Wilkinson, *Science, Religion, and the Search for Extraterrestrial Intelligence* (Oxford: Oxford University Press, 2013).

[52] Karl Rahner, "Sternenbewohner. Theologisch," in *Lexikon für*

say anything about the fact of whether or not extraterrestrials exist. The biblical sources are concerned only with the world we inhabit and its relationship with God. Christians, who profess the absolute transcendence and incomprehensible mystery of the Creator, cannot presume to claim knowledge of what God may or may not be doing in another part of the universe, or in any other possible universe. We cannot exclude the idea that life could evolve in another planetary context: Rahner says that "it would be an anthropomorphic idea that God the creator would bring the cosmic development at some other point so far that the direct possibility of conscious life would be present, but that then he would arbitrarily break off this development."[53] For Christians, then, it is appropriate to keep an open mind on the possibility of God's creative act enabling the evolution on other planets of creatures who possess self-consciousness and freedom.

If such creatures do exist, then Christian theology needs to ask a second question: May we see them as embraced by God in grace? Does God come to them in the Spirit in self-giving love? Can we expect that they too may have a history of grace? Rahner says: "One might say that it would make sense to ascribe these creatures of body and spirit a supernatural destiny immediately directed to God (notwithstanding the gratuity of grace), but we, of course, can know nothing about the presumable history of freedom of these creatures."[54] Christians believe that God's self-giving in their own history is directed toward their free human response, and ultimately to the fulfillment of the whole universe. There is no reason to exclude the idea that God's free self-giving might involve other histories of grace for intelligent and free inhabitants of other planets.

Theologie und Kirche (Freiburg: Herder 1964), 9:1061–62; "Natural Science and Reasonable Faith," 51–52; *Foundations,* 445–46.

[53] Rahner, "Natural Science and Reasonable Faith," 50.

[54] Ibid., 51.

Based on what we know of the character of God, we can say that extraterrestrials may well experience their own economy of creation and grace. We can say nothing about the history of such possible stories of grace and sin, except that we have every reason to trust that God, whom we know to be radically faithful and generous, would be so for others.

What can be said about incarnations on other planets? Rahner thinks that we need to stay open to this as a real possibility: "In view of the immutability of God in himself and the identity of the Logos with God, it cannot be proved that a multiple incarnation in different histories of salvation is absolutely unthinkable."[55] If it is possible that God is acting in many histories of salvation through the Word and the Spirit, then we would need to think of our eschatological future as embracing and bringing to fulfillment many histories of freedom in different parts of our universe:

> We would move towards the idea that the material cosmos as a whole, whose meaning and goal is the fulfillment of freedom, will one day be subsumed into the fullness of God's self-communication to the material and spiritual cosmos, and that this will happen through many histories of freedom which do not only take place on our earth.[56]

Rahner's position on God's engagement with extraterrestrials is thus a modest one. He suggests that theology should be open to their possible existence as part of God's creation, and that they might well have their own story of grace, their own incarnation, and their own participation with us in eschatological fullness. Theologians cannot know exactly how God might freely act with regard to extraterrestrials. But if God's creation

---

[55] Ibid.

[56] Rahner, *Foundations*, 445.

includes such creatures, we have good reason to trust that God also gives God's self to them in the Word and in the Spirit, with the same generous and extravagant love we encounter in our own experiences of incarnation and grace.

Rahner and Deep Incarnation: Critical Differences, Resonances, and Insights

This chapter has shown, I believe, many resonances between Karl Rahner's thought and the theology of deep incarnation, as well as Rahnerian insights that can be seen as grounding aspects of deep incarnation in the theological tradition. Some critical differences remain, however.

Critical Differences

- Although Rahner is fully explicit about salvation in Christ involving the transformation of the whole universe, in Christ, and while he sees the human as deeply interconnected with the rest of the natural world, he does not anticipate the ecological crisis is often focused on the human, and seldom on animal or plant life.
- Although Rahner's theology offers resources that can be developed in the direction of a theology of God who suffers with suffering creation, he clearly does not take this path himself.[57]

Resonances and Insights

- Rahner's overarching vision of creation and incarnation as united in one divine act of self-giving love can be seen as foundational for deep incarnation. In this trinitarian vision, God gives God's self to creation in the life-giving Spirit and in the Word made flesh in Jesus of

---

[57] See Karl Rahner, "Why Does God Allow Us to Suffer?" *TI*, 19:194–208.

Nazareth. It is divine self-giving that enables the evolutionary self-transcendence of creation. Jesus can be understood as the self-transcendence of creation to God and, at the same time, as God's radical self-bestowal to creatures.

- Rahner shares with deep incarnation the conviction that the incarnation was always the divine intention in creating a world of creatures.
- God, who is unchangeable in God's self, can change in another, in the creature. God, who is love, goes out of God's self, in love that gives itself away. God is always the fullness of love but this love is of such a kind that it can involve the freely chosen kenotic giving of self to creatures.
- Rahner comes close to a contemporary theology of deep incarnation when he sees Jesus, in his death, as entering into the very depth of the earth, "to the heart of all earthly things, where everything is connected and one, to the seat of death and earth's impermanence."[58] Jesus enters into the very heart of the earth in order to infuse it with divine resurrection life.
- Rahner parallels deep incarnation with his insistence that, in Christ, *all* is assumed, all is saved, all is to be transfigured, all is to participate in deification.
- Rahner's view of the radical unity of the one universe supports his understanding that the incarnation involves the "hypostatic union of the Logos, not just with the isolated humanity of Jesus, but with the matter of the universe as such, with the radical potentiality of the whole creation."[59]
- The risen Christ remains part of the earth and its destiny and, through his presence, the new forces of a transfigured creation are already at work conquering

---

[58] Rahner, "A Faith That Loves the Earth," 54.
[59] Rahner, "Christology in the Setting," 219.

impermanence, death, and sin at their core. Not just the church, but the creation is becoming the body of Christ.

- The resurrection is a promise of transfiguration and fulfillment not only for humans but for the whole universe of creatures: "Mother Earth has brought forth only creatures that will be transfigured, for his resurrection is the beginning of the resurrection of all flesh."[60]

- An important theme for deep incarnation is found in Rahner's conviction that the incarnation, and its culmination in resurrection and ascension, mean that God is forever a God of matter and flesh.

- Deep incarnation can embrace Rahner's argument that creatures of intelligence and love may exist on other planets with their own economy, which may possibly include the grace of the Spirit and their own incarnation of the Word.

---

[60] Rahner, "A Faith That Loves the Earth," 58.

5

The Cross

Sacrament of God's Redemptive
Suffering with Creatures

In earlier chapters I have discussed the theme of deep incarnation as it appears in the work of five evolutionary and ecological theologians, Niels Gregersen, Elizabeth Johnson, Celia Deane-Drummond, Christopher Southgate, and Richard Bauckham. Then I have taken up three of the great witnesses to a fully incarnational theology, Irenaeus of Lyons, Athanasius of Alexandria, and Karl Rahner, in order to see how their work might underpin, critique, or contribute to the development of the theology of deep incarnation.

In this final chapter I conclude with some further explorations into the theology of deep incarnation in relation to insights from the theologians already discussed. This involves taking up five theological positions: (1) it is the Holy Spirit who brings about the incarnation; (2) cosmic, evolutionary, and ecological relationships are constitutive of the Word made flesh; (3) God can be said to suffer with suffering creatures; (4) the cross of Christ is the sacrament of God's redemptive suffering with creatures; and (5) the resurrection is a promise of healing and fulfillment that embraces all creatures. I conclude with a brief reflection on two contributions that the theology of deep incarnation might bring to the discussion of Pope Francis's *Laudato Si'*.

The Holy Spirit Brings about the Incarnation

One of the characteristics of theology in recent times has been the recognition that in Western theology and church practice there has been a tendency to ignore, or to address only in a minimal way, the theology of the Holy Spirit. In response, theologians such as Yves Congar, Jürgen Moltmann, and Walter Kasper, among many others, have argued for a return to a fully pneumatological and richly trinitarian theology. Congar enunciates a fundamental axiom of this kind of theology when he says that "the Word and the Spirit do God's work together."[1] In the context of such a theological recovery of the Spirit, it would obviously be an unhelpful step if a contemporary ecological and evolutionary theology of deep incarnation were to be seen as focused only on the Word of God. Like others involved with deep incarnation, I am convinced that an evolutionary and ecological theology for our time must be a theology of the Spirit creatively at work in the emergence of the universe of creatures, as well as in all aspects of salvation in Christ. Deep incarnation needs to be a trinitarian theology of Word and Spirit.

Sharing this conviction, theologians working on deep incarnation, including Niels Gregersen, Elizabeth Johnson, and Celia Deane-Drummond, have all addressed the fundamental role of the Holy Spirit in deep incarnation. In the last three chapters I have drawn attention to key theological insights on the relation between Word and Spirit found in the theologians under discussion: to Irenaeus's conviction that God acts always by God's own two hands of the Word and the Spirit; to Athanasius's axiom that the Father creates and renews all

---

[1] Yves Congar, *The Word and the Spirit* (London: Geoffrey Chapman, 1986), 21–41.

things through the Word in the Holy Spirit; and to Karl Rahner's structuring theological principle that, in both creation and saving incarnation, God gives God's self to creatures in the Word and in the Spirit. These three principles can be brought together to say: God bestows God's very self to creatures, in creation and in new creation in Christ, through the Word and in the Spirit, the two hands of God.

The Spirit is the Breath of God who accompanies the Word of God in both creation and the work of salvation. In both, the Spirit is, as the Creed proclaims, the Giver of Life. In both, the Spirit is the one who enables creation to become what is new. The Spirit is the energy of love that enables a universe to emerge and life to evolve. The Spirit is at work, with the Word of God, in the processes that gave rise to the origin of the observable universe in the big bang, in the emergence of the primordial hydrogen and helium, in the birth of galaxies and stars, in the synthesis in these stars of further elements needed for life, in the development of our solar system around the young sun, in the origin of the first microbial life on earth, in the flowering of life in all its diversity and abundance, and eventually, in the evolution of humans with our highly developed brains, interrelated and interdependent with everything else. As Rahner has pointed out, humans emerge into a universe that is a world of grace, a world in which the Spirit is always present in self-offering love.

A systematic theology of deep incarnation will need to show how the Spirit who is the Giver of Life in creation and in grace is radically connected to the incarnation itself. It is helpful to note that this connection was already made clear by Ambrose of Milan in his *On the Holy Spirit*, published in 381. He sets out to show that the Spirit is not a creature, but fully divine, and that the creation is the work of the Spirit, whom he calls Creator Spirit. He points out that the Scriptures proclaim that the child conceived by Mary is the work of the Spirit (Lk 1:35; Mt 1:18–20). Ambrose argues from the Spirit's role in the incarnation to the Spirit's role in the creation: if the humanity of the Savior is the work of the Creator Spirit, then we should be able to see that the whole of creation is also the work of the Creator Spirit, in union with the Father and the eternal Word. Ambrose sees the Creator Spirit as the *author* of both the incarnation and the creation of the universe: "So we cannot doubt that the Spirit is Creator, whom we know as the author of the Lord's incarnation."[2] For Ambrose, then, the Spirit is the author of the whole creation, the author of the life of grace, and the author of the incarnation.[3]

Unfortunately, this theology of the Spirit was lost sight of in Scholastic theology, which attributed the grace of union between the divine and human natures of Christ simply to the Logos. Walter Kasper, among others, has corrected this with his form of "Spirit Christology."[4] He understands the Holy Spirit as the freedom and excess of divine love in person, the one who not only makes all divine action toward creatures possible, but who is also the creative and sanctifying principle at work in the incarnation. Jesus is anointed with the Spirit (Lk 4:21; Acts 10:38), who sanctifies the humanity of Jesus, so that he can be God's loving self-communication in person. The Spirit fills the humanity of Jesus and endows it with the openness by which it can freely constitute "a mould and receptacle" for God's self-communication in the Word.[5] Kasper writes that the sanctification of Jesus by the Spirit, and the outpouring upon him of the gifts of the Spirit, was not merely the *consequence* of the Logos becoming flesh in the hypostatic union, "but its *presupposition*."[6] Kasper thus reverses the Scholastic

---

[2] Ambrose of Milan, *On the Holy Spirit* 2.5.41, The Fathers of the Church Series, vol. 44 (Washington, DC: Catholic University of America Press, 2010), 110.

[3] Ibid., 117–19.

[4] Walter Kasper, *Jesus the Christ*, new ed. (London: T&T Clark, 2011), xvii.

[5] Ibid., 239.

[6] Ibid. Emphasis added.

approach. Whereas Scholasticism saw the union of the Word with the humanity of Jesus as accomplished by the Word itself, which then enabled Jesus to be Spirit-filled, Kasper holds to the biblical view that it is the Holy Spirit who brings about the birth of the Savior. And it is this Spirit who leads Jesus in every aspect of his life and ministry up to and including his death on the cross, and in and through the cross to his resurrection, which Paul tells us occurs in the power of the Spirit (Rom 1:4, 8:11).

In 1986, Pope John Paul II issued an encyclical on the Holy Spirit, one of the few formal church teaching documents on the Spirit. It is particularly relevant to the theology of deep incarnation because, in its discussion of the incarnation, John Paul II makes it clear that it is the Holy Spirit who "accomplishes" and "brings about" the grace of union in the incarnation, as the climax of the Spirit's gifts in creation and grace.[7] He points out that this grace of union is the supreme grace, the source of every other grace. His comments are important to this discussion for a second reason—he goes on immediately to describe the meaning of the incarnation which is brought about by the Spirit in words that are in agreement with key tenets of deep incarnation:

> The Incarnation of God the Son signifies the taking up into unity with God not only of human nature, but in this human nature, in a sense, of everything that is

---

[7] Referring to the incarnation, Pope John Paul II says: "It was 'brought about' by that Spirit—consubstantial with the Father and the Son—who, in the absolute mystery of the Triune God, is the Person-love, the uncreated gift, who is the eternal source of every gift that comes from God in the order of creation, the direct principle and, in a certain sense, the subject of God's self-communication in the order of grace. The mystery of the Incarnation constitutes the climax of this giving, this divine self-communication." *Dominum et Vivificantem: On the Holy Spirit in the Life of the Church and the World,* para. 50 (http://w2.vatican.va).

"flesh": the whole of humanity, the entire visible and material world. The Incarnation, then, also has a cosmic significance, a cosmic dimension. The "first-born of all creation," becoming incarnate in the individual humanity of Christ, unites himself in some way with the entire reality of the human, which is also "flesh" and in this reality with all "flesh," with the whole of creation.[8]

The incarnation signifies, we are told, "the taking up into unity with God" not only of human nature, but also of the whole of humanity, of all flesh, and of the entire visible and material world. The nature of this unity of all matter and flesh with God, at the heart of the concept of deep incarnation, is further explored in the following section.

Cosmic, Evolutionary, and Ecological Relationships as Constitutive of the Word Made Flesh

In the first chapter, I described Richard Bauckham's view of the unity of God with creatures brought about through the incarnation. Bauckham points out that God is present to creatures not only by the metaphysical presence by which God enables all creatures to exist but also in the variety of ways described in the Bible and the Christian tradition by which God freely makes God's self present in the freedom of love. Bauckham insists that the incarnation is unique, different from other forms of divine presence not simply in degree but in kind. He expresses this difference by use of the proposition *as*: God is present not only *in* or *for* Jesus of Nazareth, but *as* Jesus.

---

[8] *Dominum et Vivificantem*, para. 50. I have substituted "the human" for "man" as the translation of *homo*. The Latin text is: "*se incarnans in humanitate individua Christi, aliquo modo copulatur cum iis omnibus, quae vere sunt hominis.*"

Bauckham sees the incarnation as salvific for the whole creation in a personal and relational way. In his life and ministry, Jesus gives himself in love for other human beings and participates in interrelationships with the rest of creation. By the divine intention, in the resurrection, this relatedness is universalized, as the human particularity of Jesus is united to the divine capacity to be universally present, and the risen Christ becomes the ecological center of creation enabling all things in their interrelatedness to find their wholeness in God. Bauckham sees the incarnate Word as engaging with other species and inanimate nature in a relational and ecological way, as the risen Christ is lovingly present with all creatures in their interrelatedness. The incarnation is transformative for the whole creation because of the loving self-identification of the crucified Christ with creation, in its disharmony and decay as well as its profusion and vitality, and because the risen Christ draws the whole creation with him into the eschatological newness of resurrection.

I find Bauckham's view attractive, but I am also convinced by Gregersen's argument that deep incarnation also requires an *internal* relationship between the Word made flesh and the wider creation. He proposes that cosmic relationships are *co-constitutive* of Christ. In Gregersen's view, Jesus Christ could not be the incarnate Logos if he were not internally related to the universe of creatures. Gregersen points to what science tells us about our dependence on the atoms formed in stars, about our evolutionary history, and about our ecological interconnectedness. We cannot think of ourselves simply as individuals whose reality ends with our skins. Gregersen also points to theology, to the divine intention, where all things are created and reconciled in Christ, to argue that incarnation necessarily involves all things, so that Christ cannot be thought of as the Word incarnate apart from ecological and cosmic interconnections.

In my view, the healing and transformation of creation can be thought of as occurring through the ecological relation-

ships that Bauckham describes, but this healing and transformation of creation also require the internal connection
between creatures and the incarnate Word described by Gregersen. Pierre Teilhard de Chardin long ago pondered this
same inner interconnection between the Word made flesh
and the universe, and suggested that we may need to think
not only of the two natures of Christ, divine and human,
but also of a third nature, the cosmic nature of Christ.[9]
However, it seems simpler and fully faithful to the biblical and wider Christian tradition to take up Gregersen's
view, that the Word assumes the creaturely humanity of
Jesus with all its ecological and cosmic interconnections,
and that these interconnections are by the divine intention
co-constitutive of the Word incarnate.

I see Rahner as contributing a helpful line of thought that
supports Gregersen's position. I noted in the fourth chapter
that Rahner extends the saying of Gregory Nazianzus: "What
has not been assumed has not been healed." Rahner insists
that what has been assumed in the flesh taken by the Word is
the whole of creaturely reality. Nothing remains outside this
whole. Nothing remains outside the transfiguration and the
deification, which, beginning in Christ, draws all that exists
into the life of God. The flesh assumed in the incarnation of
the Word, is not simply the isolated individual, Jesus of Nazareth. The incarnation, Rahner says, involves a hypostatic union
of the Word with not just the isolated humanity of Jesus, but
with the matter of the universe itself, and with all its potentiality. As both Rahner and Gregersen say, the true reality of
Jesus Christ cannot be thought of as stopping at his skin. Science shows us the various ways in which we are all interconnected and interdependent in the one evolutionary and ecological whole. On top of this, theology tells us that it is by the
very intention of God that *all things* are assumed in Christ, so

---

[9] Pierre Teilhard de Chardin, *The Heart of Matter* (San Diego: Har-
court, 1978), 93.

that all things might be liberated (Rom 8:21), reconciled (Col 1:20), and recapitulated (Eph 1:20) in him.

I think Gregersen is right to say, then, that being related to the whole universe of creatures is co-constitutive of the Word made flesh. If one were to think of the Word as made flesh simply as an isolated individual, then one would miss the deep truth of incarnation. By the divine intention, the flesh assumed in the incarnation is that of Jesus of Nazareth in all its internal relationality with other human beings, with the community of life on our planet, and with the universe itself in all its dynamic processes. The flesh of Jesus is made from atoms born in the processes of nucleosynthesis in stars, and shaped by 3.7 billion years of evolution on earth. Social, ecological, and cosmic relationships are not add-ons to the Word made flesh. They are constitutive of the Word made flesh. And if one takes up the position of Irenaeus, Athanasius, Rahner, and Gregersen, then one would have to say that the creation of our cosmic, evolutionary, and ecological world was always directed to the Word made flesh. In this sense the Word made flesh can also be said to be constitutive of our interconnected and evolutionary world.

God Can Be Said to Suffer with Suffering Creatures

Can God be thought of as feeling the pain of creatures, as compassionately accompanying them, as co-suffering with them? Some theologians reject this idea, because they see it as undermining divine transcendence and the traditional view of divine impassibility. Others who support the notion of God suffering with suffering creation are quite prepared to abandon the notion of divine impassibility. I think a third response is more appropriate—the idea that we need to rethink our notion of divine transcendence and therefore of divine impassibility. Central to this third response is the idea that a God who can freely and lovingly enter into the pain of creation and feel with suffering creatures is actually more truly and fully transcendent than a God who is unable to do this. This proposal is suggested by themes I have discussed in the earlier chapters.

The theology of the incarnation and the cross found in Irenaeus and Athanasius does not support the idea of an impassive, unfeeling, and distant God. It is true, of course, that they both hold strongly to the concept of God's transcendence and impassibility. For them, God is not to be thought of as caught up in the all-too-human jealousies, lusts, and conflicts of the Greek gods or the Aeons of the Gnostic Pleroma. However, their view of God's unchanging divine nature does not mean that God is uninvolved with creation. For Irenaeus, God's *magnitudo* and God's *dilectio* are always found together. Divine transcendence is re-envisioned in the light of the incarnation and the cross of Jesus. In such a theology, a Christian notion of divine transcendence is attained only when it is qualified, in fact enlarged, by seeing it as the transcendence of divine love, as the transcendent divine capacity to be with creatures of flesh. Irenaeus's high notion of transcendence can be understood only in relation to the earthliness of the divine love expressed in the incarnation and cross of Christ. This down-to-earth, divine love, revealed in the flesh of the incarnate Word and his death on the cross, is the same love that is at work in the creation, in the hands-on making of human beings and the diverse world of creatures.

In Athanasius's view of the incarnation, the Word of God who is radically beyond all creatures condescends to be directly present to creatures out of generous, compassionate loving-kindness. As Anatolios points out, Athanasius reconstructs and transforms the idea of divine transcendence by means of the biblical categories of divine mercy and loving-kindness. In both creation and incarnation, there is a "simultaneous contrast and interplay" between two attributes of God, God as "beyond all being"[10] and God's

---

[10] Athanasius, *Against the Greeks*, 2, in *Athanasius: Contra Gentes and De Incarnatione*, ed. Robert Thomson (Oxford: Clarendon Press, 1971).

"goodness and loving-kindness."[11] Because of the divine attribute of loving-kindness, God can transcend God's own transcendence. The true nature of divine transcendence, then, is characterized by an unthinkable divine capacity for *philanthrōpia*. This kind of transcendence is far beyond inadequate human notions of transcendence that might limit God to a realm apart from creation. What Athanasius's theology transcends is a limited, finite view of divine transcendence.

In commenting on Philippians 2:5–11, Athanasius insists that this text, which speaks of the Word's humanization, cross, and exaltation, is not about the Word advancing to deification. It points, rather, to the fully divine Word who humbles himself in becoming human and accepting death on a cross. The kenotic self-humbling of the Word in the incarnation and the cross is for the sake of our advancement, that we might be raised up, and deified, as God's sons and daughters. For Athanasius this self-humbling of the Savior is not simply to be located in the humanity of Jesus, but is rather the expression of the divine nature. God's self-humbling in creation and incarnation springs from the love of the triune God and belongs to the divine nature itself. Anatolios writes that for Athanasius "a divine self-abasement is integral to the biblical character of God," and adds that "this divine humility belongs to the divine nature directly."[12] The divine nature is revealed in Christ as self-giving, self-humbling, kenotic love. This kind of love characterizes both the incarnation and the creation of a universe of creatures.

Alongside Irenaeus and Athanasius, I think it is helpful to turn to the third theologian of incarnation I have been considering in these pages, Karl Rahner. Although he never develops a theology of God suffering with creatures, I see his view of God's becoming in the incarnation as a building block for this kind of theology. Rahner asks how, in a theology of an

---

[11] Khaled Anatolios, *Athanasius* (London: Routledge, 2004), 40.

[12] Ibid., 119.

unchanging God, we might understand the central Christian conviction that the Word *became* flesh. His response is the proposal that God, who is fullness of being in God's self, and therefore unchanging, can change in another, in becoming a creature, in becoming human. The infinite God, who is pure freedom, possesses the possibility to become what is other, the finite, and to enter into the suffering of the world, above all in the cross. According to Rahner, then, the incarnation is "the *self*-emptying, the coming to be, the κένωσις and γένεσις of God himself, who can come to be by becoming another thing."[13] God is not only unchanging but can also truly become something.

What I find particularly noteworthy here is that Rahner sees this dialectical possibility of the unchanging God becoming a creature as representing, not a deficiency in God, but rather, a characteristic of a larger God. God would be less if God could *not* become other. God's transcendence, then, should not be thought of as limiting God's freedom to become a creature. Rather, a true understanding of divine transcendence would acknowledge God's freedom to give God's self in self-emptying love into the finite other. God has the possibility of freely subjecting God's self to history. All of this, Rahner points out, is about the radical nature of divine love. God, who is fullness of love, and who always remains in this fullness, can also pour out this love in self-emptying self-bestowal.[14] What Rahner says of the kenotic love of the incarnation can also apply, I maintain, to God's accompaniment of the whole creation in its evolutionary becoming. God accompanies creatures in their suffering, compassionately and redemptively.

Irenaeus, Athanasius, and Rahner all believe that God possesses the fullness of being in God's self. They all hold to the unchanging divine nature. They all hold to a strong view of divine transcendence. But in the incarnation, culminating in

---

[13] Ibid., 114.
[14] Ibid., 115.

the cross, they see God freely giving God's self in kenotic love to creatures. This means that the transcendent God has the capacity to enter into the limits and suffering of creaturely existence. As Rahner points out, this is not a diminishment of God. God is not less transcendent because God can pour God's self out in love. Those who would claim that divine transcendence means that God could not become a creature, or suffer on the cross, and, I would add, suffer with suffering creation, are in danger of using a human construct of transcendence to say what God in God's freedom may or may not do. So what we find in Irenaeus, Athanasius, and Rahner is the notion that God transcends all human notions of divine transcendence. The creation itself, and above all the incarnation and the cross, mean we need to enlarge our view of transcendence. A purely philosophical view of transcendence is inadequate. We need a bigger picture of divine transcendence, because God is love, the radical fullness of love, a love that can also pour itself out kenotically in a world of creatures. It is this kind of love, I am proposing, that is at work not only in the incarnation and the cross but also in the emergence of the universe and the evolution of life on earth with all its terrible costs and in all its wonderful outcomes. It is this kind of love, and this kind of transcendence, that enables us to claim that God accompanies creatures in their suffering, feeling with them out of the divine capacity for compassionate love, and redemptively suffering with them.

The Cross as Sacrament of God's Redemptive Suffering with Creatures

Having argued that God can and does suffer with creatures in their diminishment and pain, I want to propose now that the cross of Jesus can be understood as the sacrament of God's redemptive suffering with creatures. In the first chapter I referred to Gregersen's proposal that the cross of Jesus can be understood as "an *icon* of God's redemptive co-suffering with

all sentient life as well as with the victims of social competition." He also speaks of the cross as the *exemplar,* and the
reality, of a God who enters into suffering and bears the costs
of evolution, and as the *microcosm* in which the suffering of
the macrocosm is represented and lived out. In each of these
concepts, the cross functions like an effective symbol, where
what is symbolized is brought about. In a broadly catholic
theology this kind of symbolic structure is usually understood
in sacramental terms.

I think it is worth recalling Rahner's sacramental understanding of the cross at this point. His questions were different
from those addressed by deep incarnation. He was seeking an
understanding of salvation in Christ that might avoid the problems of forensic atonement theologies. In particular, he wanted
to avoid any suggestion that the cross changes God's mind,
or pacifies an angry God. He wanted to show that salvation
springs from God, from God's love and from God's saving will.
He thought that any attempt at a renewed theology of salvation
in Christ would still need to answer the fundamental question
of how we are saved through the cross. How is the cross the
cause of our salvation?[15] Rahner also faced a second major issue
in his theology: because he had long argued that saving grace
is offered to every person of every time, he needed to show the
proper connection between this universal offer of saving grace
and the Word incarnate in Jesus Christ. If saving grace is present
and offered to every person, including those who lived before
the life and death of Jesus, what is the meaning of the Christian
belief that we are saved by the cross of Christ?[16]

Rahner's response is to propose that the cross of Christ is
the sacramental cause of our salvation.[17] In doing so he builds

---

[15] See Karl Rahner, *Foundations of Christian Faith: An Introduction
to the Idea of Christianity* (New York: Crossroad, 1978, 1995), 283–85.

[16] See ibid., 316–18.

[17] Rahner writes: "The life and death of Jesus taken together, then,
are the 'cause' of God's salvific will (to the extent that these two things

on his major work on "The Theology of the Symbol" where he writes of the incarnate Word as "the absolute symbol of God in the world, filled as nothing else can be, with what is symbolized."[18] Rahner sees reality as symbolic, and God's very being as symbolic—the eternal Logos is the real-symbol, the symbolic self-expression of the Source of All; the Word made flesh is the real-symbol, the self-expression and self-giving of God to the world of creatures. Rahner insists that this concept of symbol is far removed from a mere sign, where what is signified has no inner relationship to the sign. A real-symbol, or sacrament, is the self-expression of what is signified, and it is effective. It not only represents, but it also brings about what is signified. The cross, the whole Christ event, constitutes a new situation of salvation in our world. But it does not override human freedom. Humans, Rahner insists, participate by grace in their own salvation. They are free to accept or reject what is offered to them. They participate by their embrace of the love poured out on the cross, and by being conformed to Christ, and becoming part of his Body.

When Rahner describes the relationship between the cross and salvation in sacramental terms, the cross, of course, involves the whole event of the Word made flesh, the self-giving love of his life and ministry, which culminates in his death, and is intrinsically connected in his resurrection. As

---

are regarded as different) in so far as this salvific will establishes itself really and irrevocably in this life and death, in other words, in so far as the life and death of Jesus, or the death that recapitulates and culminates the life, possess a causality of a quasi-sacramental and real-symbolic nature. In this causality what is signified, in this case God's salvific will, posits the sign, in this case the death of Jesus along with his resurrection, and in and through the sign it causes what is signified" (ibid., 284). Rahner uses "quasi-sacramental," presumably, simply to distinguish this use of the language of sacramentality from its related use of the church itself, and of the sacraments of the church.

[18] Karl Rahner, "The Theology of the Symbol," in *Theological Investigations* (New York: Crossroad, 1982), 4:221–52.

the culmination of the self-giving love of the life of Jesus, and as including God's acceptance of this self-giving in the resurrection, the cross of Christ is the explicit, bodily symbol and the reality in our world of divine mercy and forgiving love. It expresses God's will to bring all into the divine life, and this saving will becomes effective in and through the cross.

Salvation is indeed poured out in the cross. But the saving effects of the cross are already quietly at work throughout the world and throughout history, in the Spirit. This Spirit, Rahner insists, is always the Spirit of Jesus Christ. The grace encountered in the Spirit is always the grace of the incarnate Word and his cross. The effects of the cross are not confined to the period after the cross, but are already present and at work, even if obscurely, throughout all of history in the Spirit of Jesus Christ.[19]

In an insightful and compelling work on Rahner's soteriology, Brandon Peterson demonstrates how Rahner's theology of the cross is grounded in his early wide and deep reading of patristic theology, above all in Irenaeus's theology of recapitulation of all things in Christ.[20] Peterson makes a convincing case that Rahner's theology of the cross is not only *sacramental* but also *representative*. Rahner's representative soteriology, Brandon shows, possesses three characteristics: (1) it centers on Christ's person, and on personal union with him; (2) it has a descending, incarnational character—as Athanasius taught, God became a human that we humans might become God; and (3) it has an ascending character—Christ is the authentic

---

[19] In this sense, Rahner notes, Jesus's incarnation and cross are the final cause of the Spirit at work throughout history (*Foundations*, 317–18).

[20] Brandon Peterson, *Being Salvation: Atonement and Soteriology in the Theology of Karl Rahner* (Minneapolis: Fortress Press, 2017), particularly 1–48, 211–62. Other important studies on Rahner's symbolic theology include Joseph Wong, *Logos-Symbol in the Christology of Karl Rahner* (Rome: LAS, 1984), and Stephen Fields, *Being as Symbol: On the Origins and Development of Karl Rahner's Metaphysics* (Washington, DC: Georgetown University Press, 2000).

human before God, Paul's and Irenaeus's "new Adam," the one in whom we participate. In this view, redemption is both objective and subjective. Christ himself is objective redemption. Subjective redemption occurs by relationship to him and incorporation into his Body. Peterson shows that Rahner's theology can only be understood as a sacramental theology of salvation that is also a representative theology, and that each of these two categories implies the other. Jesus Christ is shown to be constitutive of salvation, as salvation itself, and our participation in salvation is understood in relational terms as union with Christ.

Rahner, in attempting to deal with a fundamental effect of the cross, namely the grace that is salvific for humanity, proposes a fully sacramental relationship between the cross of Jesus Christ and the grace of the Spirit at work throughout human history. I think it can be said that the proponents of deep incarnation are taking up a further meaning and effect of the cross, namely God's loving and redemptive solidarity with suffering creatures, and proposing an iconic or sacramental relationship between the cross and God's redemptive co-suffering with suffering creatures. In a theology of deep incarnation, then, the meaning of the cross is *both* God's forgiving and transforming grace for human beings and God's entering freely and lovingly into the pain and the drama of existence of all creatures. In this vision, redemption in Christ involves *both* forgiveness and life for human beings and God's loving accompaniment and redemptive embrace of suffering creatures. For both of these meanings, there is a sacramental relationship between the cross of Jesus as the explicit expression, and the reality, which is saving grace for human beings through relationship with Christ, on the one hand, and the Word's compassionate and loving presence in the Spirit to all suffering creatures, on the other.

In my view it is important and helpful, in thinking about the cross as sacrament of God's redemptive suffering with the whole creation, to remember the ways in which the cross functions as sacrament of God's redemptive presence to Christians in their suffering. The symbol of the cross is at work everywhere in the Christian tradition, and it is certainly true that it often represents divine forgiveness and saving grace for human beings in their sinfulness. At other times, however, it functions in the second way described above. In extreme suffering, and in nearness to death, for example, many Christians look on the cross, or hold the cross, or kiss the cross, and know God's compassionate, loving, and strengthening presence with them, and something of the promise of resurrection life. In such cases, I think it can be said that the cross of Christ is not only functioning as a symbol of divine forgiveness but also as a sacrament of God's loving presence and redemptive co-suffering.

The sacramental, iconic relationship between the cross of Christ and the universal work of the Spirit already exists in theology and church life. It exists in the theology of grace and in the way the cross functions for many Christians in their suffering and death. What the proponents of deep incarnation seek can be understood as an extension of this sacramental structure, so that the cross of Jesus is understood more explicitly as the sacrament of God's redemptive co-suffering with all creatures.

I find resonances in this sacramental understanding of the cross with Irenaeus's vision of the cross, described in chapter 2, where he sees the cross as inscribed across the whole creation, reaching across the sky and into the depths of the earth. The cross is imprinted by the Word on the whole of reality, and in the depths of reality. The Word of creation, the Word who is creatively present to all creatures, is revealed fully and visibly in the cross. The love poured out on the cross is the visible expression of the Word's love at work everywhere in creation. The cross makes fully visible the cruciform activity of the Word of God, who acts invisibly in the height and in the depth, in the length and in the breadth of all creaturely reality.[21] There

---

[21] Irenaeus, *Demonstration,* in *St. Irenaeus of Lyons: On the Apos-*

are resonances, too, in the sacramental understanding of deep incarnation, with Athanasius's strong conviction, discussed in chapter 3, that the Word of the cross is the Word of creation, and with his reflection on Matthew's account of the cross, where the whole creation participates in Jesus's death, as the earth shakes and the mountains are split. Athanasius observes that creation was not silent at the death of the Word on the cross, but, rather, "the whole of creation was confessing that he who was known and suffered in the body was not simply a man, but the Son of God and Saviour of all."[22]

In the twenty-first century, a theology of the cross as sacrament of God's redemptive suffering with suffering creatures can enable us to say that the love poured out in the incarnation of the Word, which culminates in the cross of Jesus, can enable us to affirm the compassionate presence of God to all the creatures of our evolutionary world. It can enable us to speak of a God who accompanies creatures in their groaning, and promises their participation in liberation and fulfillment in Christ.

Resurrection:
A Promise of Healing and
Fulfillment That Embraces All Creatures

In my view, the promise given in the resurrection of Christ is essential to deep incarnation. It is not enough to say that God is lovingly present with suffering sentient creatures. Both God suffering with creatures and the resurrection promise to them are essential to deep incarnation. In fact, I agree with Christopher Southgate when he says that a theological response to the costs of evolution involves at least four elements. He calls

---

tolic Preaching, trans. John Behr (Crestwood, NY: St. Vladimir's Seminary Press, 1997), 34.

[22] Athanasius, *On the Incarnation*, in *Athanasius: Contra Gentes and De Incarnatione*, 19.

this a "compound theodicy."[23] My own, slightly different, way of speaking of Southgate's four elements is to propose that a theological response to the suffering of God's creatures needs to involve at least four theological positions: (1) we are evolutionary creatures in an evolutionary universe, created by God in a noninterventionist way that respects the proper autonomy of natural processes;[24] (2) God can be thought of as feeling the pain of creatures, as compassionately accompanying them and redemptively co-suffering with them; (3) the promise of the resurrection is that "the creation itself will be set free from its bondage to decay and will obtain the freedom of the glory of the children of God" (Rom 8:18–25); and (4) human beings are called to participate in God's love and action toward the wider creation in an ecological commitment to the healing and flourishing of the planetary community of life. Like Southgate, I think that each of these elements is necessary for a response to the loss and suffering built into the creation and that all are needed for a theology of deep incarnation.

The third of these elements, the hope of resurrection, has been built into the theology of deep incarnation from its begin-

---

[23] Christopher Southgate, *The Groaning of Creation: God, Evolution and the Problem of Evil* (Louisville, KY: Westminster John Knox Press, 2008); "Does God's Care Make Any Difference? Theological Reflections on the Suffering of God's Creatures," in *Christian Faith and the Earth: Current Paths and Emerging Horizons in Ecotheology*, ed. Ernst M. Conradie, Sigurd Bergmann, Celia Deane-Drummond, and Denis Edwards (London: Bloomsbury, 2014), 97–114. I differ from Southgate when he proposes that the *only way* that God could create our kind of finite world is through evolutionary processes with their built-in costs, because I think that like Job, we stand before the incomprehensible, and cannot claim any kind of full knowledge of why God creates in the way God does. This element of negative theology means that I describe my reflections on the suffering of creation simply as a theological response rather than as a theodicy.

[24] I have discussed the noninterventionist nature of divine action in *How God Acts: Creation, Redemption, and Special Divine Action* (Minneapolis: Fortress, 2010).

ning, even if it has not always been fully developed. Without the risen Christ there can be no theology of deep incarnation. Gregersen has always seen the presence of God to suffering creatures as actively transforming suffering and bringing life, and he clearly holds to the promise of resurrection life for the whole creation. At this point I note a difference in emphasis between Gregersen's view and my own. In his criticism of simplistically historical and chronological approaches to incarnation and resurrection, Gregersen makes a strong claim that the Logos was always embodied. He recognizes that from our limited historical and temporal framework, what we can say is simply that the Logos was always meant to become incarnate in Jesus. But from the perspective of the divine life, Gregersen says, there never was and never will be a disembodied Logos. There never was a divine life without Christ knowing suffering and death from within—the Lamb is "slain from the foundation of the world" (Rev 13:8).

I find myself cautious about the claim that the Logos was always embodied. For one thing, I am not sure that we can say very much about the life of God from the divine perspective. I tend to think we are limited to what we can know from our creaturely and time-bound perspective, even as we admit that God's eternal perspective is far beyond our own. The concept of incarnation involves God embracing time and history, and accepting and respecting historical limits, which leads me to think that the theology of deep incarnation might well do the same. I am conscious of the way Irenaeus, Athanasius, and Rahner envision the one economy of creation and salvation as united in the one divine intention, but as taking place only in time, in history, and reaching its fulfillment only in God. Each of them thinks that something radically new happens in the incarnation. Rahner insists that the Word of God *became* flesh. At a certain point in our human history, and in the history of the universe, the Word of God became a creature, became something new. It is hard to grasp the wonder and novelty of this act of God, if one also says that the Word was eternally flesh. I am inclined, then, to interpret the Lamb slain before the foundation of the world as referring to the Wisdom/Word of God who was always to become flesh and embrace suffering and death in order to bring healing and life to creation.

This line of thought can find support in the work of Celia Deane-Drummond and her concept of deep incarnation as theo-drama. Such a dramatic approach to the incarnation brings out the particular way that the Word of God is embedded in the frail, bodily, and mortal Jesus of Nazareth. It brings out the specificity and contingency of his life and of his death on a cross, and the way this drama is grounded in the divine life of the Trinity. In a theo-dramatic view the incarnation is understood as the dramatic in-breaking of divine love in our world. For Deane-Drummond, the theo-drama of Christ's life and death opens out in the dramatic event of resurrection, so that Christ's death and resurrection can be seen as fully inclusive in scope, "widening out to the universal reach of God's love shown in Christ to all creatures."[25]

My view of the universal reach of the resurrection is grounded in the range of New Testament texts that speak of the creation and reconciliation of *all things* in Christ (1 Cor 8:6; Rom 8:18–25; Col 1:15–20; Eph 1:9–10, 20–23; Heb 1:2–3; 2 Pet 3:13; Jn 1:1–14; Rev 5:13–14, 21:1–5, 22:13). A theology of deep resurrection can build further on the views of Irenaeus, Athanasius, and Rahner discussed in the last three chapters, all of whom see the wider creation as participating with human beings in the final transfiguration in God of the whole of creaturely reality. I am convinced, however, that we can have no clear comprehension or any accurate imaginative picture of the future of all things in God, because the future of

---

[25] Celia Deane-Drummond, "The Wisdom of Fools: A Theo-Dramatic Interpretation of Deep Incarnation," in *Incarnation: On the Scope and Depth of Christology*, ed. Niels Gregersen (Minneapolis: Fortress, 2015), 200–201.

all creatures, including that of human beings, is in the incomprehensible mystery of God. What we have is not a clear picture, but an unbreakable promise of God in the resurrection of the crucified Christ. Based on the character of God revealed in the incarnate one, in his life and ministry, and his cross, as self-giving love, we can trust that God not only sustains and cares about every sparrow (Mt 10:29; Lk 12:6), but also will bring each of them to redemptive fullness in a way known to God. Based on the revelation of divine love found in Jesus, we can trust that each species and each individual living creature will find its place in the divine communion.

The fullness of redemption in Christ, I am suggesting, can be understood as a deifying transformation in three radically interrelated aspects of created reality: (1) with regard to *matter*, the incarnation, and its culmination in resurrection, is the beginning of the transfiguration of the universe, with all its processes and entities, the beginning of its glorification and fulfillment; (2) with regard to *biological life*, the biblical promise is for the final liberation and fulfillment in Christ of "the creation itself" (Rom 8:19), and for the recapitulation (Eph 1:10) and reconciliation (Col 1:20) of "all things" in him, and this includes, in some unforeseeable way, other species and individual creatures; and (3) with regard to *humanity*, it involves the forgiveness of sin, the indwelling of the Holy Spirit, and becoming God's beloved daughter or son, resurrection life, and communion with the whole creation in the life of the Trinity.

God embraces "flesh" in Jesus of Nazareth, so that creatures of flesh might be transformed and taken fully into communion with the living God. Because of what we know of the character of God revealed in the incarnation, it is safe to argue that this transformation will be appropriate and proper to each creature and each species. This flesh that is transformed includes each kangaroo, each dolphin, as well as each sparrow, in ways that are appropriate to each. They are created through the eternal Wisdom of God, and participate in some real way in redemption and reconciliation in Christ through the Spirit of God who dwells in them. In the Word made flesh, God embraces the whole of life on earth, with all its evolutionary processes, in an event that is both a radical identification in love and an unbreakable promise.

Deep Incarnation as Contribution to *Laudato Si'*

Given the state of our planet, given the climate change we already experience, given the devastating loss of species, given the terrible burden of ecological disasters on the poorest people of earth, I think Pope Francis's *Laudato Si'* may well be the most important church document of the twenty-first century. At its heart is the idea that we are called to an ecological conversion that involves an indivisible commitment to suffering humanity and to the community of life on earth. Francis insists that earth is our common home, that everything is interrelated and interdependent, and that we are all kin, participants in a sublime communion of creation.

Laudato Si' offers a remarkable theology of the natural world. Instead of an often-taught Christian view of the natural world as given simply for human use, it proclaims that other creatures, and ecosystems, have their own intrinsic value before God. Three reasons are offered in the encyclical for this intrinsic value: God holds each creature in love; God is present interiorly to each of them; and each of them is to participate with human beings in God's final transformation of all things. Francis sees the natural world as revelatory of God, a book of God alongside the book of Scripture.

Laudato Si' is a document that theologians need to learn from, discuss, and seek to develop theologically. The theology of deep incarnation, in my view, offers two key insights that have the capacity to augment the theology of *Laudato Si'*. The first concerns the systematic place of incarnation for a theology of creation, and the second is concerned with a theological response to what might be called the negative side of our evolutionary existence.

The Systematic Theology of Incarnation

The central theological vision of creation in *Laudato Si'* is found in its second chapter, the "Gospel of Creation." In this chapter, Pope Francis turns to the Bible to articulate a theology of the whole of creation as one interrelated community before God. There is much that is said here that is powerful and important, but it is largely a creation theology drawn from the First Testament, with some reference at the end of the chapter to New Testament creation texts. *Laudato Si'* is already a long document that could not do everything. Later in the encyclical Francis writes of the risen Christ as present to the whole creation and as bringing the universe of creatures to its fulfillment. Referring to Colossians 1:19–20 and 1 Corinthians 15:28, he says: "Thus the creatures of this world no longer appear to us under merely natural guise because the risen One is mysteriously holding them to himself and directing them towards fullness as their end. The very flowers of the field and the birds which his human eyes contemplated and admired are now imbued with his radiant presence" (para. 100). Later he writes: "Christ has taken unto himself this material world and now, risen, is intimately present to each being, surrounding it with his affection and penetrating it with his light" (para. 221). In discussing the sacraments (para. 235) and the Eucharist (para. 23), Francis offers brief comment on the theology of incarnation in relation to ecology.

It is clear that Pope Francis's insights depend on an incarnational theology, but there is no attempt to develop such a theology in *Laudato Si'*, or to show structural links between creation and incarnation. The Prologue to the Gospel of John is mentioned in paragraph 99, but the encyclical nowhere develops a systematic theology of the Word of creation and incarnation. Such links are made in the theology discussed in these chapters, in the work of Irenaeus, Athanasius, and Rahner, and are developed explicitly, and in new ways, in the theology of deep incarnation of Niels Gregersen, Richard Bauckham, Celia Deane-Drummond, and Elizabeth Johnson, among others. In my view, the theology of deep incarnation can offer a theological underpinning for the prophetic teaching of *Laudato Si'*, and is a needed and appropriate development of its theology.

The Negative and Violent Side of Creation

Laudato Si' does not address the costs of evolution that are built into the process: the loss, the pain, the predation, the deaths, and most of the extinctions of species that have ever lived over the 3.8-billion-year history of life. There is little acknowledgment of the violence of the natural world. Again, it is entirely understandable that *Laudato Si'* could not do everything. But I see it as essential for Christian theology, in engaging with this extremely important teaching text, to address the issue of the negative side of nature, and the costs that are part of it.

This issue is sharply focused in Pope Francis's beautiful discussion of the experience of God in nature. He writes: "The entire material universe speaks of God's love, his boundless affection for us. Soil, water, mountains: everything is, as it were, a caress of God" (para. 84). He embraces the ancient tradition of the book of nature: God has written a precious book, "whose letters are the multitude of created things present in the universe" (para. 85). He says: "From panoramic vistas to the tiniest living form, nature is a constant source of wonder and awe. It is also a continuing revelation of the divine" (para. 85). In another context he says simply: "Nature is filled with words of love" (para. 225). I find these texts inspiring and challenging.

I believe it is essential, however, to add to them the idea that nature can confront us in ways that seem ruthless and cruel. Human beings and creatures of many other species suffer greatly from natural events such as earthquakes and tsunamis as well as from human violence. Gregersen is right, then, to point out that while God is universally present to creatures, not all events reveal God in the same way. As Gregersen says, God is omnipresent, but not omni-manifest. God is not clearly *revealed* in all the processes of natural selection, as God is not revealed in a concentration camp, but God is *present* in natural selection and in the horror of a concentration camp. God is not absent from those who suffer from natural and human horrors, but radically present with them and for them, as accompanying, compassionate love and promise.

In beautiful and deeply meaningful expressions, Pope Francis says that there are times when the natural world can be experienced as the *caress* of God, and as *speaking words of love* to us. Deep incarnation adds that there are also aspects of the natural world that involve terrible loss and great suffering. It insists, however, that even in events of horror God is present in love as faithful, loving companion in our creaturely suffering and as promise of life. Perhaps the most important insight of deep incarnation is that the cross of Jesus, the Word made flesh, is the icon, or as I have said here, the sacrament of God's redemptive co-suffering with creatures who endure horrors, and as promise of their participation in the healing and transfiguration of resurrection life.

I conclude this exploration of deep incarnation with words of Pope Francis that express the hope of deep resurrection in aesthetic terms:

At the end, we will find ourselves face to face with the infinite beauty of God (cf. 1 Cor 13:12), and be able to read with admiration and happiness the mystery of the universe, which with us will share in unending plenitude. . . . Eternal life will be a shared experience of awe, in which each creature, resplendently transfigured, will take its rightful place and have something to give those poor men and women who will have been liberated once and for all.[26]

---

[26] Pope Francis, *Laudato Si'*, para. 243.

Index